The many first-person stories make this book so approachable and lifelike, with imperfect attitudes much like my own. I llove the memorable and unique image of the Castellers, too!
— Erin Healy, editor, bestselling novelist
Colorado Springs, CO

Tight and loaded with lovely quotes, leads for other material and practical examples that give traction in people's lives … all the stuff I love in a book. I will readily hand this off to others.
— Penn Clark, author, international conference speaker
Penn Yan, NY

WOW! This is really, really thought-provoking stuff with practical application in how we parent, lead and grow others.
— Les Herron, pastor and life coach
Houston, TX

Easy to read, with lots of treasures and practical applications. It put words on things that we are practicing by intuition.
— Joële Z.eller, International Leadership Team of KKI
Yverdon, Switzerland

3G

The art of living beyond your life

How to pass on your hard-earned values so next generations start on your shoulders, not under your feet.

CURTIS CLEWETT

Published in the USA and UK.

Ordering Information:
Additional copies of this edition can be ordered at any Amazon website in the US or in Europe.

Requests for multiple copies of this book may be directed to:
3gthebook@gmail.com

Clewett, Curtis L.
3G: The Art of Living Beyond Your Life.

ISBN-13: 978-1976210488
ISBN-10: 1976210488

Edition 1a

Cover design: Karen Carrera

Table of Contents

Preface

My wife, Patti, and I currently live in Spain, where we have raised four children and been privileged to lead a youth outreach program called King's Kids for over twenty-five years. (You'll read more about how we got into this amazing work with an innocent name in Chapter 3.)

Some time ago, while traveling across the US, we heard one too many stories of a colleague's child gone bad. These were kids of our friends, some far more virtuous than us. It hurt and scared us to think this might be the fate of our own family. Our children seemed to be doing reasonably well. No one was into drugs. They still enjoyed going out on ministry service trips with us. But it was time for a reality check!

Somewhere in southern Oregon, we stopped the van, locked the doors, and declared a family meeting with our offspring—now a captive audience. Patti got right to the point.

"All right, you guys! Are each of you still committed to keeping the faith? Are you doing okay? Is there anything going on that we should know about?" After receiving assurance that there wasn't an evil Mr. Hyde alter-ego lurking in their lives, I asked, "So what have we done or not done as parents that has prevented you from following your friends into a destructive lifestyle?"

Our oldest daughter, Kari, blurted out, "Family vacations!"

Family vacations? I had been hoping for something like "great parenting," "correct discipline," "excellent role model," or some other pat on the back. But family vacations?

Kari explained how those times—away from the press of other responsibilities, telling stories without checking our watches for another appointment—helped build her identity as a Clewett. The answer surprised us and got us thinking. We put the key back into the ignition and started a new journey toward understanding a 3G, or third-generation, lifestyle.

We began teaching about 3G in 2010 at conferences and gatherings in Europe and other parts of the world. We were consistently met by tearful and grateful singles who no longer feared getting married; parents who found encouragement, hope and a plan; as well as ministry and business leaders determined to adopt a 3G leadership style. Many asked if we could write down our ideas in book form. What you hold in your hands is the result.

Introduction

Is it possible to live beyond the end of your life?

Before we get too metaphysical, ask yourself this question: What are the key values and core beliefs that shape your existence? Is there a way to deeply stamp these into the lives of your succeeding generations, literally extending your life beyond physical death?

The answer is yes! In fact, there is a simple plan recorded in the recesses of the Old Testament Scriptures that tells us how:

> *These words, which I am commanding you today, shall be on your heart. You shall teach them diligently to your sons and shall talk of them when you sit in your house and when you walk by the way and when you lie down and when you rise up. You shall bind them as a sign on your hand and they shall be as frontals on your forehead. You shall write them on the doorposts of your house and on your gates. (Deuteronomy 6:6-9)*

Sounds too easy, doesn't it? All we have to do is connect even the most mundane moments—going to bed and getting up, going out or chilling at home—to eternal principles and keep these core values visible. A word for this process is *discipleship*. It's the method Jesus used to train up twelve world-disruptors. Asking deep questions about ordinary stuff is how the great Greek philosophers passed on their revolutionary thoughts to succeeding generations. Abraham laid a foundation of unrelenting faith in his posterity that still affects us today. Finding out how they did it and how you can start leaving a legacy for your succeeding generations— whether children, followers or friends—is the intent of this book.

Some may think they have nothing to pass on. A 44-year-old divorced man with no kids asks: "What can I possibly leave to future generations?"

Plenty! Everyone has a set of hard-earned lessons, principles fire-tested in real life, that are worth handing over to the next in line. Everyone in a relationship with other human beings is influencing them for better or for worse. Why not be intentional about influencing for the better?

3G is based on taking the long view of your relationships. It's not about controlling your posterity, but rather releasing them to influence a third generation (3G) and even more.

3G living not only *affects* but *infects* the people close to you. You're not just teaching but transmitting the vital principles that define you, your family or your organization.

The essential ideas of 3G living could be summed up in three statements:

1. **Experience life together.**

2. **Intentionally evaluate experiences, connecting them to underlying values.**

3. **Delegate responsibility early.**

The concept is simple, but the application is not easy in our electronically isolated twenty-first-century lifestyles.

After reading an early draft of *3G,* an author friend

cautioned from a parent's perspective:

Most parents I know worry about whether we are parenting well. We carry a lot of guilt and a sense of failure. Our culture has come to believe that all childhood problems can be prevented with astute parenting, and the reason there are so many problems today is because parents basically stink. So most of us walk around discouraged, under heavy burdens or with defensive attitudes. Of course we hope that our parenting will be good enough to impact future generations positively, but to be frank, we'll be glad if we can just launch our own kids well. To think even that accomplishment might be a failure is almost too much to bear. I felt something within me want to withdraw from the perceived pressure to do and be more [after first reading the 3G draft].

Good point! Her comments spurred an extensive review of the manuscript to make sure this is a book about hope, not guilt, encouragement, not condemnation!

If you are a desperate parent, or a discouraged leader, please don't give up! In Chapter 12, you'll read testimonies of failed leaders and sorrowful parents who are clawing their way back into relationships with estranged children and resentful co-workers. Skip to that chapter now if you need a quick shot of encouragement!

Most of the material in this book is not new. It's more like a cobbled scrapbook of brown-paged thoughts from wiser people, seasoned by Bible clippings and contoured by our own 3G learning curve.

Having served in Christian ministry circles for four decades, I will unapologetically appeal to biblical authority to establish key lines of thought. If the reader doesn't share my faith perspective, please patiently persevere and consider references from authorities you respect. I am convinced that these principles are universal. My prayer is that the ideas considered in these pages will be helpful, no matter your philosophical or religious persuasion.

Chapter endnotes have been restricted to quotes, statistics and thoughts that are not my own. More scholarly references could have been included. But one of the great discoveries on our journey has been the power of stories to humanize and connect emotions to logical constructs. A quote attributed to Einstein:

> *If you want your children to be smart, tell them stories. If you want them to be really smart, tell them more stories. If you want your children to be brilliant, tell them even more stories.[1]*

We could paraphrase and say, "If you want your second generation to capture values, tell them stories." I hope you enjoy this folksy aspect of the book. (And I also hope I don't embarrass our kids or my wife too much in the process!)

-Curtis Clewett, Barcelona, September 1, 2017

---

[1] http://www.azquotes.com/quote/876064

CHAPTER ONE

Are We Generationally Nearsighted?

Live and don't learn.

-Collected wisdom from Calvin and Hobbes

Generations—we all belong to one.

A generation defines a group of people born within a given set of years, sharing common history and certain characteristics. Sociologists name them "Boomers," "Generation X" or "Millennials." Marketers exploit them: "The Pepsi Generation." And historians link them to trends and technologies: "The Facebook Generation."

A generation may experience a spiritual awakening or may sink to depravation of biblical proportions. Yet, more often than not, the ideals that make one generation great will perish with its last survivor. Sacrifice and compassion forged by economic depression are lost on children who never suffered. The courage and resilience of those who fought in great wars become a distant memory to those who have only known peace.

What will be the epitaph of your generation, and more specifically, of your life? "It was good while it lasted," with not a trace of enduring values visible in your children and grandchildren, or in the lives of people you influence? I hope not!

However, having worked with families and leadership teams for decades, one thing has become painfully clear: good parents can raise wayward children, and good leaders can produce poor followers.

Can it happen to me? It happened to Samuel!

Samuel: The 1G Giant

Samuel, a monumental Old Testament figure, led the children of Israel out of a dark age back into light. Few have been more faithful. He was spotless in character, an exemplary leader. Yet at the end of his life, the young Israelite nation rejected Samuel's prophetic leadership line, choosing instead to install a monarchy and follow a king. Why?

Most people who know Samuel's history will answer, "to be like the other nations around them" or something similar. This may be true but doesn't tell the whole story. Why did they reject his posterity to lead them? Here's the devastating answer:

> *And it came about when Samuel was old that he appointed his sons judges over Israel ... His sons, however, did not walk in his ways, but turned aside after dishonest gain and took bribes and perverted justice. Then all the elders of Israel gathered together and came to Samuel at Ramah; and they said to him, "Behold, you have grown old, and your sons do not walk in your*

*ways. Now appoint a king for us to judge us like
all the nations." (1 Samuel 8:1, 3- 5)*

Wow! Did you catch that? Samuel's kids were brats! Somehow, in the daily crush of judging the people, listening to God and doing good, there wasn't enough time left over to raise his sons. The result: everything built up in one generation was lost to the next. *His legacy did not make it past his lifetime!*

Samuel's tragic example must be understood. We could call him an extraordinary "1G" or one-generation leader. He had a giant influence solely over his own generation, not the next. He probably believed that if he lived life well, God, or maybe inertia, would somehow raise his family. He was mistaken, as unfortunately are so many families today.

I wonder sometimes if we, like Samuel, are growing generationally nearsighted. We act based on what's good for now, in this lifetime. The Scriptures often reveal a much longer view of our life's purpose. Observe the divine mandate to invest in succeeding generations:

> *These words, which I am commanding you
> today, shall be on your heart. You shall teach
> them diligently to your sons and shall talk of
> them when you sit in your house and when you
> walk by the way and when you lie down and
> when you rise up. (Deuteronomy 6:6-7)*

His plan goes even further:

> *Tell your sons about it, And let your sons tell
> their sons, and their sons the next generation.
> (Joel 1:3)*

The Scriptures are filled with references to generational sequences, warnings, stories and results of how acts of individuals can affect lives for millennia to come. Here's just a sample of both the good and the bad of generational transmission:

Third and Fourth Generation

I, the LORD your God, am a jealous God, visiting the iniquity of the fathers on the children, on the third and the fourth generations of those who hate Me." (Exodus 20:5)

Tenth Generation

No Ammonite or Moabite shall enter the assembly of the LORD; none of their descendants, even to the tenth generation, shall ever enter the assembly of the LORD. (Deuteronomy 23:3-4)

Thousandth Generation

Know therefore that the LORD your God, He is God, the faithful God, who keeps His covenant and His lovingkindness to a thousandth generation with those who love Him and keep His commandments. (Deuteronomy 7:9)

All Generations

Your faithfulness continues throughout all generations. (Psalm 119:90)

Can you see the pattern? Our lives are not islands with defined coasts, at least not from the Creator's viewpoint.

Rather, we are a part of a much longer story, continuing the narrative of previous generations and purposed to influence the generations that follow. The decisions you make and what you do today

> Our lives are not islands with defined coasts, at least not from the Creator's viewpoint.

affects the destiny of people living far beyond your lifetime.

This is 3G thinking: considering how to invest values and principles into the next generation so they can do the same for the third generation and potentially the next and the next.

A Swiss banker first introduced me to this idea years ago in a seminar about personal finances. He started by quoting this Proverb:

> *A good man leaves an inheritance to his children's children. (Proverbs 13:22)*

He challenged us to make economic decisions according to how they would affect our children and even grandchildren. Do you rent or do you buy? Should you get that new car on credit or save to purchase in cash? He made a strong case that our financial lives are not our own. We need to handle our resources considering how our choices will affect our posterity.

The idea of looking at life's decisions through a generational lens began to bang around my head like a pair of old sneakers in a washing machine. Like many, my primary focus was on survival, making ends meet, staying reasonably optimistic and trying to be kind. Yes, we had kids and spent quite a bit of time disciplining and instructing them. Surely that's an investment in the second generation! But were they understanding what was behind our decision not to let them go to the discotheque at age fourteen, or to require them to ask forgiveness for an offense at school? Maybe we were doing a good job controlling them now, but were they capturing these values to guide their own decisions in the future and someday even be able to pass them on to their children and people they influence?

I remember a day in third grade when I could not read the text in the filmstrip (anyone remember that technology?) in the darkened classroom. No amount of squinting helped. I needed glasses! I was so embarrassed. The teacher had to practically drag me to the eye exam to confirm my nearsightedness. I could focus clearly on things up close, but they were blurry just a few feet away. Corrective lenses overcame myopia, but it took a while to get over my self-consciousness!

Are we nearsighted when it comes to considering our lives through a divine generational lens? Are we content to focus all our energy on the good, bad and ugly of our own lifetime, or are we also taking into account the third and even fourth generations to come?

Perhaps some will sigh at this point, like my author friend quoted in the introduction. All this can sound like a burden too heavy to bear for those struggling just to survive in the present, much less think about fifty years down the road. However, a slight change in perspective can actually lighten the load! Hang on and keep reading. The path is about to get brighter!

Speaking of eye problems, almost eighty percent of the population in urban areas like Guangzhou, China, suffer from myopia, nearsightedness, while in rural Nepal less than one percent have it. Where they don't squint at TV and mobile phone screens, where they focus on objects mostly farther away, their eyes work better. [2] *Fascinating!*

So, let's put on our "glasses" and go back a few millennia to see how others passed on values from one generation to another. We will begin by examining the legacy of two different four-generational sequences. The first represents a pattern of thought forged over a two-hundred year span that forever altered Western civilization's way of looking at itself. The second example is a biological family, from great-grandparents to great-grandchildren, that chipped a stubborn faith out of Middle Eastern deserts and still challenges us thousands of years later. In each of these histories, a core set of beliefs was received, protected and passed on through three generations, resulting in a surprising fourth.

* * * * * * * * * * *

questions for reflection

- *What are two or three positive values you have inherited from your parents or a key leader in your life?*

- *How does your family history relate to the story of Samuel referred to in this chapter?*

- *Think for a moment about your close followers or children. What are some of the things they do to mimic you, maybe even without knowing it? What does this say about passing on characteristics to your next generation?*

chapter one endnotes

[2] Robert Wojciechowski, *Clinical Genetics*- http://www.ncbi.nlm.nih.gov/pmc/articles/PMC3058260/

CHAPTER TWO

Fourth Generation is the Charm

The Greek Connection

The twelve young men were still waiting for class to begin on the grassy slopes of *Academy*, the outdoor site of Socrates' school for elite Athenian sons, when the thirteenth student straggled in. Aristocles, the teacher's pet, was late almost as often as their professor. Now, in the hot morning sun, he was trying to squeeze his huge frame into the last piece of shade when his tunic caught on a rock, ripping through the white fabric, and setting off a storm of laughter. He was so big and clumsy. No wonder they called him "Plato" ("the broad one").[3]

Chasing the laughter away with threats to pulverize the smaller boys and jokes to placate the older ones, Plato concentrated on today's task. His master, Socrates, insisted on a method of questioning. Not just multiple-choice questions to be answered a, b or c, but questions about, well, everything! Socrates didn't teach concepts like other highly paid professors of the day, but rather engaged his students in constant

> He (Socrates) claimed to be more like a midwife than a professor, coaxing out truth that is already in each of us.

question-and-answer drills. He claimed to be more like a midwife than a professor, coaxing out truth that is already in each of us. Plato was a good questioner, one of the best, but he still couldn't seem to pin his teacher down to a straight answer about anything. Socrates always answered with another question. To top it off, Socrates never wrote down his teachings. How was Plato supposed to study, and how could he master ideas that were never stated, only questioned?

Well, today would be different. He was armed! Plato had prepared a battery of questions that would demand an answer.

"Professor, may I ask you something?" Plato tested.

"Certainly!" replied the professor. "And what would be your question?"

"A friend of mine, Hippothelas, has composed songs of glory to himself before winning the actual battle. Would you consider him prideful?"

"All right," replied Socrates. "What should you say of a hunter who frightened away his prey, and made the capture of the animals which he is hunting more difficult?"

"Uh, I suppose he would be a bad hunter," Plato stuttered.

"Yes. And if, instead of soothing them, he were to infuriate them with words and songs, that would show a great want of wit, do you not agree?" probed Socrates.

"Yes, I suppose so," answered Plato while muttering under his breath, "It's gonna be another long day!"[4]

Socrates was a disruptive thinker and generally considered the Father of Western Philosophy. Plato, his star student, would refine and systematize Socrates' teachings, eventually becoming head of the *Academy*. He memorialized his mentor's method into a series of written "dialogues" where the characters would question each other over things real and abstract, launching the reader into logical and philosophical query. The "Socratic Method" and Plato's "Dialogues" are still foundational for training lawyers, politicians and critical thinkers today.[5]

Plato had a star student of his own named Aristotle, whose musings about math, physics, astronomy, rhetoric, biology and logic laid the foundations for these scientific fields and many more.[6]

Those who remember their high school history and philosophy classes will easily recognize this three-generation sequence: Socrates, Plato and Aristotle. Each one was deeply affected by the life and passions of the preceding mentor, inheriting a "love of wisdom," which is the literal definition of philosophy.[7]

Now, here comes the surprise. Who was Aristotle's star student?

You may know him by the name of...Alexander the Great, perhaps the most brilliant military strategist of all time. Philip II, King of Macedon, placed his son, Alexander, in Aristotle's school. The young crown prince devoured Aristotle's approach to life, his philosophy, the epic tales of ancient heroes and moral stories intertwined with Greek mythology. Still a young man at twenty-one years old, Alexander gathered up a few classmates from the Academy and set out on a mythic journey of his own, conquering an area of about two million square miles across three continents by outfoxing armies and subduing civilizations many times greater than his native Macedonia, before his death at age thirty-two. His biographers tell us that Alexander slept with nothing but a dagger and a copy of Homer's *Iliad* under his pillow at night.[8]

Three generations, each building upon the knowledge and wisdom of the former, produced a mega-talented conqueror in the fourth. The point is not that Alexander was somehow better or more principled than others or even that Aristotle approved of his pupil morphing into a "military philosopher" that killed and enslaved simply for the glory of conquest. Rather, this is a clear illustration of how a philosophy or way of life can be transmitted, amplified and polished through multiple generations, birthing leaders who can literally change the world.

The Israeli Connection

Abraham's roots were anything but what we today might call "Christian." Born by the name of Abram (meaning "little Father" in Hebrew), he was raised in Ur of the Chaldees, near Nasiriyah in the southeastern part of modern Iraq. Joshua tells us that Abram's family "served other gods."[9] They were basically idol worshippers.[10]

Genesis 12 records Abram's first encounter with Yahweh, a God unknown to the Chaldeans, that would forever change his religious convictions and those of countless millions after him.

> *Now the LORD said to Abram, "Go forth from your country, And from your relatives And from your father's house, To the land which I will show you; And I will make you a great nation, And I will bless you, And make your name great; And so you shall be a blessing; And I will bless those who bless you, And the one who curses you I will curse. And in you all the families of the earth will be blessed." (Genesis 12:1-3)*

Abram had something in his character that lit up the divine radar.[11] He possessed an unshakable confidence, an unusual capacity for trust and a willingness to follow this new God into...what? To the "land which I will show you." One celestial encounter was all it took to leave his family and culture, change geography and change religion! The Bible singles him out as a shining example of "faith."[12]

Can you imagine Abram's friends and relatives, watching him take down his tent and pack up his family, asking him the obvious question, "Uh, Abram, we see you're getting ready to leave. Exactly where are you going, again?" and his answer, "I really don't know. This new God you've never heard of will show me when I get there." You can predict the ridicule of his hearers.

But Abram does go, despite what other members of his clan may have thought. He travels over a thousand miles of desert, trusting that Yahweh knows what He is doing. Along the way, he sees his kidnapped nephew miraculously recovered,[13] believes God for a naturally born child at one hundred years old,[14] and has his name changed to Abraham ("Father of Nations") as God seals His covenant with a man He called His friend.[15]

Three world religions—Judaism, Islam and Christianity— look to Abraham as their father. He was given the honor of being Yahweh's first last name ("God of *Abraham*, Isaac and Jacob").[16] Abraham possessed a kind of faith that produced obedience even to the point of sacrificing his miracle son, Isaac, on Mount Moriah.[17] Abraham and God were "tight." Like Samuel, Abraham was a great leader. But unlike Samuel, Abraham was able to pass on key character traits to his children.

Abraham, of course, was not perfect! He had problems telling the truth, as you'll see in chapter five. But for now, let's look into a couple of instances where Abraham's faith was transmitted effectively to the next generation.

First, we must understand that Hebrew customs and traditions were passed on orally. Storytelling has always been a part of Jewish culture[18] (and should become a part of *our* heritage-passing to the next generation). Isaac's name in Hebrew, *Yitzhak*, literally means "laughter." You can bet the hilarious tale of his birth to a ninety-year-old woman, and other stories of Abraham's God-encounters, were told often around the family fire on cold desert nights, imprinting a sense of identity and belonging on his young heart.

The Bible does not shed much more light on Isaac's early upbringing until he was summoned to accompany his father to Mount Moriah. God had told Abraham to sacrifice Isaac on a mountain shown to him. Going somewhere without being told why was nothing new for Abraham. But to sacrifice his miracle son must have seemed a staggering contradiction.

First of all, he was being asked to murder his own child. Human sacrifice was common in the surrounding nations of his time, but far from the character of the merciful and righteous Yahweh he was coming to know. An even greater paradox was how God would keep His promise to bless the nations through Isaac if Isaac was dead. Good question!

We won't spend more time here exploring the backstory of this unusual request, which Jewish tradition calls the *akedah*,[19] the last of Abraham's ten tests of faith. For our purposes, we note that father and son experienced this defining moment *together*. Finally, instead of just hearing stories of courage and faith, Isaac would live this one out (barely!) with his father. So what exactly happened?

Although some traditions place Isaac as a child, he was almost certainly between the ages of seventeen and thirty-five,[20] old enough to carry the firewood for the sacrifice, and old enough to understand that something highly irregular was going on. Genesis only records one conversation between them. Isaac asks, "Behold, the fire and the wood, but where is the lamb for the burnt offering?" Abraham responds, "God will provide for Himself the lamb for the burnt offering, my son." [21] Surely there were more exchanges during their three-day hike to Moriah. How were the fish biting on the Jordan River? Which potential brides might be good candidates for Isaac? How was the local football team doing? We really don't know what they said, but almost every father/son odyssey includes questions asked and lessons learned along the way. Sometimes these are even more important than the actual event. We will spend quite a bit of time talking about these "teachable moments" of values transmission later.

Abraham and Isaac come to the mountain, separated from the accompanying servants, and Isaac suddenly realizes that he will be the sacrificial lamb to be drawn and quartered, then burned on the altar they were constructing. Here's what happens next:

> *Abraham said to his young men, "Stay here with the donkey, and I and the lad will go over there; and we will worship and return to you." Abraham took the wood of the burnt offering and laid it on Isaac his son, and he took in his hand the fire and the knife. So the two of them walked on together. (Genesis 22:5-6)*

Now here is the strange part: Isaac didn't argue or fight. Strong enough to carry the wood, old enough to understand how this sacrifice thing worked, Isaac simply walked with his father to certain death. How could he do that?

Part of the answer may lie in Abraham's explanation to the servants: *"I and the lad will go over there; and we will worship and return to you."* Notice he said, "we." He was not coming back without Isaac. The book of Hebrews lends a clue to what apparently was going through Abraham's mind:

> *By faith Abraham, when he was tested, offered up Isaac...of whom it was said, "Through Isaac shall your offspring be named." He considered that God was able even to raise him from the dead, from which, figuratively speaking, he did receive him back. (Hebrews 11:17-19 ESV)*

We can only guess Isaac's thoughts as they walked up the hill, stepping over thorny Palestinian scrub, and spending hours gathering rocks for an altar. But after having heard countless stories and witnessed perhaps twenty years of his father's unflinching obedience to God's commands, Isaac simply walked on. The word was sure, the decision was made. That was enough for him. Now, he was writing his own story of trust, shaping with his father another stone in the foundation of faith that still serves us today, some two hundred generations later!

Abraham, Isaac, Jacob—a familiar trio. Three generations, each building on the other. And the fourth? Ever hear of a guy named Joseph?

Joseph was sold to slave traders by his brothers, falsely accused and imprisoned. Not an easy start! Yet he possessed a unique gift and a solid faith that propelled him to became the de facto governor of Egypt, second only to Pharaoh. As supreme authority over food distribution during a famine, his influence stretched far beyond the shores of the Nile.

Let's take one last glance at these incredible generational sequences:

1G: Socrates

2G: Plato

3G: Aristotle

—> Alexander the Great

1G: Abraham

2G: Isaac

3G: Jacob

—> Joseph

Three generations shape a set of values and convictions that produce a world-class leader in the fourth. Was it coincidental, or can we discover keys that preserved and perfected ideas and faith through one generation to another?

We will see this pattern of third- and fourth-generational influence repeatedly as we explore how to live a 3G lifestyle.

But first, a little bit of our own story.

* * * * * * * * * *

questions for reflection

- *Think about your potential fourth generation. What are two of your core values you would like to see multiplied in your great-grandchildren or fourth-generation followers? What would it look like? Describe somethings they would do, how they would react in given situations.*

- *How will you go about modeling and establishing these values for your second generation? (If stumped, don't worry! Following chapters will give you tools!)*

chapter two endnotes

3 According to C J Rowe, *Plato* (1984).

4 Adapted from Plato's Dialogue *Lysis* (translated by Benjamin Jowett. New York, C. Scribner's Sons (1871).

5 see http://www.law.uchicago.edu/prospectives/lifeofthemind/socraticmethod

6 see *Aristotle*, http://www.philosophers.co.uk/aristotle.html

7 In Greek: *sophia* = wisdom and *philo* = love.

8 Robin Lane Fox, *Alexander the Great*, (2004) p 59

9 *Joshua said to all the people, "Thus says the LORD, the God of Israel, 'From ancient times your fathers lived beyond the River, namely, Terah, the father of Abraham and the father of Nahor, and they served other gods.'" (Joshua 24:2)*

10 *We can make some educated guesses about their religion by looking at the history and religious artifacts from that period. Ur of the Chaldees was an ancient city that flourished until about 300 BC. The great ziggurat of Ur was built by Ur-Nammu around 2100 BC and was dedicated to Nanna, the supreme moon deity of their pantheon of gods. -What was Abraham's Religion before God Called Him?* http://www.gotquestions.org/Abraham-religion.html.

[11] 2 Chronicles 16:9 describes God's scan of earth's inhabitants that can easily be compared with our modern radar systems: *For the eyes of the LORD move to and fro throughout the earth that He may strongly support those whose heart is completely His.*

[12] *By Faith Abraham, when he was called, obeyed by going out to a place which he was to receive for an inheritance; and he went out not knowing where he was going. (Hebrews 11:8).*

[13] *Genesis 14:11-16.*

[14] *Genesis chapters 17-18.*

[15] *"But you, Israel, My servant, Jacob whom I have chosen, Descendant of Abraham My friend." (Isaiah 41:8).*

[16] *See Exodus 3:6.*

[17] *"There is some archaeological evidence to suppose that the place of the crucifixion of Jesus was at the summit of Mt. Moriah, probably near the present-day Damascus Gate and the Garden Tomb which would of course be a literal fulfillment of Abraham's offering of Isaac when God said, "On the mount of the Lord it [the final offering for sin] will be provided." Mount Moriah, Site of the Temple Mount in Jerusalem.* http://www.templemount.org/morih2.html.

[18] See *Storytelling and Spirituality in Judaism,* http://www.hasidicstories.com/Articles/Hasidic_Theories/spirit.html.

[19] Literally "binding" in Hebrew, signifying Abraham's binding of Isaac.

[20] *How Old was Isaac when God Asked Abraham to Sacrifice Him?* http://www.biblestudy.org/question/how-old-was-issac-when-god-asked-abraham-to-sacrifice-him.html.

[21] *Genesis 22:7-8.*

Our 3G Story Begins

Life is what happens while you're making other plans.

-*John Lennon*

My wife, Patti, and I landed in Barcelona, Spain in 1991, a year before the Olympics, with three children in tow and ready to start a second-half-of-life adventure. Five years earlier we were running a successful business in Ventura, California, with a Jacuzzi in the backyard and nice wheels in the garage. Both of us had been involved in missions and youth work in the past and we were getting bored with the American Dream. I know that sounds odd. But making a little bit more money to have a little bit better place to live in a little bit nicer area...it doesn't compare to vital involvement in the transformation of entire lives through simple acts of service, counsel and care that are the bread and butter of charitable work.

I had been in Spain many years earlier on a teenage service outreach. Perhaps we could be a point of light in that nation with less than one half of one percent Evangelical Christians and a rapidly receding Catholic Church, dented from three decades of a Franco quasi-religious dictatorship. We were thirty-six years old with nothing to prove and the best years of our lives waiting to be lived. Our business inventory was sold off and now, here we were!

We began leading a few seminars about music, leadership and family, subjects where perhaps we had something worth sharing. However, we quickly discovered that Spanish leaders weren't so anxious to hear what North Americans have to say. We tend to be pushy, brash and even rude with our know-it-all attitude and insensitivity to local culture (I found out later!)

Opportunities thinned for the higher-level training I had expected among pastors and mission leaders, but they opened up dramatically in another area: youth! Patti and I had both been youth pastors before but surely we had graduated from that! No longer young and never having been cool, I was more than ready to let others work with the juvenile set. I was prepared for "real" adult ministry, not babysitting kids! Nonetheless, an international youth ministry with an innocent name was about to jolt our paradigm.

In 1992 I helped lead a large multinational outreach at the Olympic Games in Barcelona. We had the finest Christian rock bands, sports teams, and pantomime groups from around the world. They spread out all over the city performing open-air concerts, doing service projects and sharing about their faith. One of the participating groups was called King's Kids, International, a ministry of Youth With A Mission. They brought an impressive three thousand people to the outreach. Their teams consisted of a few adults but mostly teenagers, preteens and even children, all in matching T-shirts! Most sported some kind of music and choreographed dance program for their outreach, and few spoke Spanish. "What possible impact could they have on our 'Christian-averse' city?" I thought to myself.

One of my jobs was to go around to the one hundred and seven outreach locations around Barcelona (it was a big outreach!) and see how teams were doing. I would offer help interpreting and connecting with local pastors. Everywhere a King's Kids team was operating, crowds were bigger and the ambience was warm and friendly. The kids were easily breaking through our city's hermetic resistance to *sectas* (the Spanish epithet for any non-Catholic religious persuasion, including Evangelicals). Swedes, Americans, Filipinos, Dutch, Brazilians—it didn't matter where they were from or how bad the sound system was, they were getting through while more "professional" outreach teams were struggling. I was fascinated but also glad that my season for youth ministry was over. While contemplating the spectacle of young people singing, dancing and sharing their personal testimonies in the streets, I accidentally uttered the seven words you should never say out loud:

Seven words you should never say out loud: "Somebody ought to do something about that."

"Somebody ought to do something about that."

Never say that! You know why? Because that "somebody" *just might be you*!

I was impressed. Different ages sharing the Good News (what we call "evangelism") on the streets was a great idea. Somebody should do something about that. Somebody should take it further. Upon reflection, I should have said, "A non-North American person under age thirty, not last-named Clewett, ought to do something about this." That would have exempted me, and the following decades would have turned out quite differently.

What I didn't realize was that this ministry wasn't really about singing and dancing at all (some groups had amazing levels of performance, while others weren't that good). Their music and turns at the microphone were merely a byproduct of other things taking place outside of public view. These multi-generational teams contemplated and discussed timeless truths in morning quiet times, then learned to resolve conflicts, asking forgiveness for frictions arising from living 24/7 on the move for three to six weeks. Somewhere in the process—here it is—values were being passed down from older to younger while living them out in real time together! It was a discipling community, not unlike the way Jesus trained his motley crew of twelve. Team members were learning by experiencing and then evaluating together on site. Their classroom was Barcelona, and the results were astonishing.

I thought I knew how to work with young people: prepare good teachings, do fun stuff, and keep them from breaking furniture or getting the girls pregnant until they grow up to be "real" members of their society and their church. King's Kids was different. These young people were not just spectators but protagonists, experiencing their faith on a whole new level. "Somebody ought to do something about that."

A few months later a group of leaders asked me to start a King's Kids group in Barcelona. I agreed to supervise but not lead—after all, I had graduated from youth and children's ministry, right? I said if they could find six Spanish parents (six other "somebodies"), I could get them started while spending my best energy on more important things like producing radio programs, starting small groups and speaking in churches.

They found six other Spanish parents, and we headed off on a twenty-five-year adventure that would launch four thousand young people into truly incredible mission adventures around the world. We are indebted to Dale and Carol Kauffman, the founders of King's Kids (now called KKI) and the many international leaders who patiently helped a hard-headed American understand the principles behind what he saw on those warm Olympic afternoons in 1992.

In the coming chapters, we will walk gingerly into the minefield of subjects like family life, raising children and leading people. I can't pretend to be an expert in all these fields, only a pilgrim with a few observations learned along the way. However, I did once produce Spanish language radio programs for *Focus on the Family*, and founder Dr. James Dobson is a bona fide expert. Talking about raising a next generation, specifically teenagers, he is fond of saying:

> *"When I graduated with my doctorate in Family Therapy, I had something like twenty-five laws for raising teens. After a few years of practice, my list was reduced to fifteen guidelines. Ten years of listening to heartbreaking stories of family trauma impossible to mend, I was down to five suggestions. Now, I say to parents of teenagers, 'Just get 'em through it!'"* [22]

There is no magic formula. Passing values through to a second and third generation is not some parlor trick with directions inside the box. It demands hard work, intentional conversations, and probably inconvenient changes to your present lifestyle. The results are never certain. However, the potential is enormous. Is there an Isaac, Jacob, and perhaps even a Joseph in your future?

* * * * * * * * * * *

questions for reflection

- *What are some goofy language mistakes or cultural missteps you or someone you know have made while visiting a foreign country?*

- *What is a "wrong" in the world about which "somebody ought to do something?" How would you like to be involved in righting that wrong?*

chapter three endnotes

[22] http://www.drjamesdobson.org/popupplayer?
broadcastId=e72d7853-1d63-4d30-b7c6-5394c0c3f52c

3G: Experience Life Together, Debrief, Release

The unexamined life is not worth living.

-Socrates

Living 3G means learning to focus on what those around you have *caught*, not just what they were *taught*.

Success is determined by how values are received by your second generation. If they are capable and passionate about passing them along to the third generation, then you've lit the match. If you have done your job well, it might even provide a strong platform for a fourth go-round, a Joseph or Alexander generation, where these convictions are now second nature, giving them confidence to push past immovable barriers and become world changers.

So how do we do this 3G thing? Let's begin by contrasting 1G, 2G and 3G lifestyles, pointing out the differences and similarities.

Contrasting 1G, 2G and 3G Lifestyles

A 1G lifestyle focuses on self: what's good for me, meets my needs or feeds my vices. 1G slogans could be: "He who dies with the most toys wins," "I'm looking out for number one," "Do what I say, not what I do!" 1Gers can be hurting, like the depressed mom strung out on cocaine. She may have good reasons for her habit, but her offspring will pay the price with probable birth defects or worse. 1Gers can be negligent, like the working dad whose occasional beers after work morphs into an alcoholic nightmare. They can be selfish, like the young single deciding to crash his or her life into as many drugs, sexual partners and pleasurable stimuli as possible, losing an inward reason for living in the midst of outward "success." Or, —surprise—they can be selfless, like the busy social worker who brags about never taking a vacation because of too many important things to do, while his family breaks at the seams and he doesn't even have time to notice. (Remember Samuel?) The common factor? Too busy doing stuff to think about training and developing their progeny.

2G people, on the other hand, do have a desire to impact posterity. However, their methods often are more about controlling than releasing. Their strategy is to somehow protect their children or students from the evil world. 2G parents may build up means to make sure their kids will never go hungry or suffer the way they did. They believe that good teaching and the power of their own example is enough. A 2Ger could be a successful businessperson who creates a huge trust fund and can't understand why his or her offspring never develop a strong work ethic. Perhaps they are parents who have learned the value of hospitality and are clueless as to why their kids resent outsiders constantly intruding into their family space. 2Gers can be soft or tough, faith-motivated or greedy. They may be admired or despised by those who know them best. Their lives may *affect* but will rarely *infect* the next generation.

2G leaders can also err on the side of leniency, believing that the fewer rules there are in the family or workplace, the more creative their children and workers will be. This *laissez faire* style of leadership can be misleading. While people need space to be creative, they also need boundaries and evaluation moments of connecting values to their behavior. "Live and let live" sounds up-to-date and politically correct, but people raised under this regimen have no clue about best practices or excellence in what they do. They never know when they have done a good job or when their work needs improvement. 2G progeny must reinvent the wheel in each generation. They are deprived of the lessons learned by earlier generations. They must start on the ground, not on the shoulders of their forebears.

Most of us fall into this 2G category. We are motivated to see change in the people we influence, but our teaching methods fall short. Consider the biblical example of David: a man of sterling character, faith and leadership. He prepared Solomon with everything needed to reign well. Great 2G job, David! But what happened in the third generation? Solomon's son, Rehoboam, lost everything in the first few days of his reign, tearing the Israelite kingdom into pieces that have never been fully reunited.[23]

The Discipleship Key

To understand 3G living, it's important to consider three different ways of transmitting information as shown in the triangle illustration (figure 1).

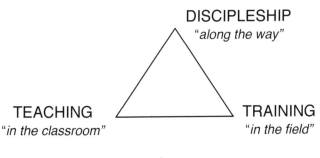

figure 1

One method is teaching. Teaching occurs in a classroom setting where one person with knowledge attempts to transfer that understanding into the minds and notebooks of their students. They may use visual aids or allow questions, but communication is mostly one-way. The relationship is teacher to student. The student learns by hearing and seeing. It works well for abstract issues like math or history. Results are measured by exams.

Another method is training. This occurs in the field. If you want to learn how to ski, it won't happen in the classroom! You must go out to the slopes, get used to your feet sliding out from under you, shiver in the cold, fall down a given number of times and keep practicing that wedge turn until, miraculously, you make it down the hill in one piece! Your instructor does some teaching, but mostly he leads by example, watches how you do it and then suggests corrections. The relationship is instructor to novice. Both must be actively involved in the training process. You learn by doing. This method is vital for building practical skills. Results are measured by demonstrated ability.

A third method is discipleship, and this happens along the way. When a Jewish rabbi deemed a student sufficiently worthy to learn under his tutelage, he simply said, "*Leck hackeri,"* or "Follow me." For the next fifteen years, that is exactly what his disciples did: follow. They learned to eat the way he ate, speak the way he spoke. It was all a matter of imitation. If the rabbi had a limp, his disciples learned to walk with a limp. If he ate left-handed they became southpaws. (I'm not making this up![24]) Teaching, when it occurred, was question-and-answer, many times related to actual events they were watching or doing together. A rabbi's particular worldview and way of doing things was called his "yoke."

Bible students will recognize this as Jesus' way of training his twelve disciples. He was fond of saying, "Take my yoke upon you and learn of me."[25] The apostle Paul captured this method nicely: "Be imitators of me, just as I also am of Christ."[26] The relationship is mentor to disciple, and learning is a combination of hearing, observing and doing.

Figure 2 below is a table outlining these three methods of learning.

method	**Teaching**	**Training**	**Discipling**
Where?	in classroom	in the field	along the way
Relation	teacher to student	instructor to novice	mentor to apprentice
Learn by	hearing	doing	hearing and doing
Results	exams	demonstrated ability	character transformation

figure 2

This is certainly the best, if not the only, way to transmit and establish values in a next generation. The key additional element—beyond written exams, beyond skills testing—is experiencing life together. Constant formal and informal evaluation happens in the course of their journeys. As important as it was for Jesus' disciples to hear his teaching about seeds planted in four types of soil, the discussion afterward taught them the true meaning of the parable of the sower.[27] Their classroom was anywhere at any time. The results speak for themselves.

My dad was a great discipler in many respects. We Clewett kids learned a lot about integrity watching him go back to the store counter and return the extra change mistakenly given out by the salesperson. We observed him honor everyone in introductions. He would pick up stray soft-drink cans and trash along public walkways. His princely example in public and private traced an indelible pattern in our lives. I don't remember him ever saying, "This is how you should treat people." Perhaps it would have sealed in those values even better. But part one of discipleship—example—was definitely there. He also exemplified how to cheat in cards and a few other vices, but that's how it works. You let people into the private parts of your life, and they see the good, the bad and even the ugly.

So, 3G has everything to do with discipleship. Shared experiences and storytelling trump lectures and exams when we talk about shaping character. 3Gers know the importance of modeling best practices. Yet they have also learned that *example is not enough*. There must occur times of evaluation and debriefing, going over what happened, leading their disciples into "aha!" moments. They borrow heavily from the question-and-answer techniques of Socrates and Jesus. They artfully capture "teachable moments" that happen along the way. Even the most embarrassing and awkward occasions become launching pads for value reinforcement.

On the dusty road to Capernaum, the disciples began to argue about who was the greatest. Jesus innocently asked them, "Hey what were you guys talking about back there?" Peter, normally the spokesman, suddenly had a mute mouth and the moment became a masterclass on servant-leadership.[28] Abraham and Isaac's Mount Moriah experience sears a powerful image of the coming Messiah into Israel's history. Plato's frustration becomes the foundation stone for the legal profession.

Sounds great, doesn't it? So what's the catch? Why don't our children, protégés and "disciples" always capture our passion?

Two difficult words come to mind: time and involvement. Shared experiences are the bedrock of 3G. However, when both parents work, and mealtime becomes an a la carte snack with each person glued to an electronic device, where does shared experience fit in a 21st-century setting? Natural teachable moments like fixing cars together or cooking meals with a child are few and far between.

> Two difficult words come to mind: Time and involvement.

How can business leaders and managers project a 3G lifestyle in a downsized workplace where results take precedence over relationships? Video conferencing and electronic communication make meetings more efficient but also delete natural storytelling moments where employees and co-workers can catch the "why" behind what we do, during downtimes on shared business trips or in between meetings.

We simply don't have time or are too exhausted to recognize and respond to teachable moments. (Typical family teachable moment: five-year-old tugs on mom's skirt while she's ordering takeout on her mobile and asks, "Momma, where do babies come from?" Typical response, "Go ask your father!") We forfeit our value formation to trending media and social networks, and our families and organizations are paying a price. We need to make room for experiencing life together if we are going to experience 3G results.

I remember our first official King's Kids outreach in 1993. We brought in a couple of twenty-somethings from Switzerland who knew how to "do King's Kids" to help us plan a camp and outreach. They taught us seven or eight choreographed songs. We learned how to do things like "heart checks"—times of asking forgiveness and straightening out any bad attitudes before performances on our tour of plazas and parks along the coast of Catalonia in the northeast triangle of Spain. Once we got started, however, the reality of trying to control a group of twenty to thirty youth aged ten to nineteen began to dampen our enthusiasm. They wouldn't go to sleep at night. They acted like, well, kids! They were not exactly the young spiritual giants that this ministry was supposed to produce. Mental sanity slowly drained away from sleep-deprived adult leaders.

Yes, people responded favorably to our renditions of "This Little Light of Mine" in the plazas and parks, but I didn't really get it. How were these unruly preteen boys, letting lizards loose in the girls' room in the morning and fighting over who got the biggest cookie at lunchtime, supposed to become amazing presenters in the evening performances?

Our learning curve was steep. Accustomed to weekend youth services where we had two hours to knock some sense into restless hormone-driven young hearts, we didn't manage a 24/7 environment with these guys very well. We knew how to keep control by making young people conform to our adult world of quiet, information-driven learning. But we were clueless about releasing: creating a learning environment where youth could experience and evaluate what was going on around them. I think my wife asked me at least three times for the keys to the car to go home and leave me in the midst of this chaos.

Things came to a head when one of our leaders suggested we take the kids to jail. "Not a bad idea," I thought, until he clarified. The idea was not to drop them off for safekeeping, but to do a performance for the inmates. As final authority on this outing, I pondered what would happen if anything went wrong. We didn't have permission slips. It wasn't on our official agenda. Thoughts of finding myself in striped pajamas behind bars flashed across my mental marquee. I tried to maintain a positive spin on what seemed an outrageous plan and told the guy, "Look, we don't even know where the jails are in this area and I don't have time to find out. Take the car. Drive into the next town. If you can find the jail and somehow get permission to perform, we'll go. You've got two hours." Feeling absolutely Solomonic in my decision, I watched them drive off and finished my breakfast. About an hour later, they were back. Great! Surely they got lost or discouraged. Nope!

"You're never gonna believe what happened." The young man beamed. "We were driving around, couldn't find a phone book or anyone who knew anything about a jail. Finally we parked and prayed. When we looked up, we noticed a sign in front of the gray building across the street: *Centre Penitenciari de Catalunya!*" You can probably guess the translation. It was the district prison! Before I could even enunciate, "Oh, no!"

> Things came to a head when one of our leaders suggested we take the kids to jail!

there was more. "And," he continued, "the warden not only invited us to come, but called up his friend who runs another jail a half hour farther away, and they want us there as well!"

Double "Oh, no!"

His eyes were a pair of spirit-fired gas lanterns. I couldn't put them out with a bucket of prudent reasoning why this wouldn't work, could I?

"Uh, that's great!" I stammered. "When do they want us to come?" I asked, hoping for a major schedule conflict.

"Tomorrow at ten o'clock. And they're even offering us some food!" Not fair! The warden had seduced them with something no young person can resist!

The next day we split the team up and headed out to the *Centres Penitenciaris* of Girona and Figueres. I'll never forget that feeling of bars clanging shut behind my back as we entered the jail. I had a camera around my neck to record this probable disaster (and to exonerate me in case everything went south). One of the prison workers told me to hide it because pictures were, of course, not allowed. I told him I would just take photos of the kids.

Our first song went well. In fact we received a shocking, thunderous applause. However, it was our second piece that reminded us where we were. We had prepared a sketch about forgiveness. A businessman sits down on a park bench. He gets distracted reading the newspaper, a thief steals his briefcase and runs off stage. Before we could move on to the good part about forgiveness and reconciliation, the two hundred or so inmates clapped a huge applause—for the thief! Not exactly what we expected! Twenty minutes later we were done with our program. Now what?

In public places we generally send out the young people two-by-two to talk with bystanders, starting up conversations with questions: "Did you like the program? Have you ever seen anything like this before?" Should we do this now? We're talking about a medium-security facility with rapists and murderers sprawled on plastic chairs in an open courtyard. We sent our kids out to talk to them.

My eyes still water and my chin trembles as I write this. Hardened cons started crying. Sentence-servers began sharing their life stories and begging the young people to pray for them and their families. A preteen pulled on my shirtsleeve and asked for help because one of the inmates wanted to know how to receive this hope he saw in their young hearts. All the adults were in shock, while the kids just assumed this was normal. At the end of our time, a group of prisoners saw my camera and insisted I take their picture together with the young people. They wanted a souvenir to send to their own wives and children. Something was clearly happening beyond our control.

Not until later, during our debriefing time, did we begin to understand what was going on. How many times had parents and teachers warned these young people not to behave badly or else someday they might wind up in jail? How many times had they been exhorted by well-meaning Sunday school teachers that they were the light of the world and had a hope within them that others longed to possess? In less than an hour, they had not only gone to jail—that awful destination of "bad people"—but had experienced up-close and personal how these guys embraced the simplicity of their emergent faith. We adults witnessed a living illustration of what it means to "Permit the children to come to Me; do not hinder them; for the kingdom of God belongs to such as these."[29] Eighteen young people and five adult leaders had just shared a 3G experience!

Someone once said there are three kinds of people in this world: those that make things happen, those that watch things happen and those that wonder what happened! 3G is about building the first category of people.

It was not easy to plan and execute that first tour. It cost money, robbed vacation time we might have spent lounging on a beautiful Spanish beach, and we literally ended up sitting in jail! It was uncomfortable yet exhilarating and destroyed me for more. There were real risks and potential for disaster, awkwardness and even failure, but we were learning that's all part of the package if you want to turn spectators into protagonists.

To say it clearly, 3G living will cost time and involvement and may require changes in your schedule and mindset. Values are *caught* not *taught*. Transmission happens in teachable moments along the way. If our lifestyles never place us "along the way" with those we are trying to influence, how can they catch our most precious possession?

> If our lifestyles never place us "along the way," with those we are trying to influence, how can they catch our most precious possession?

It's impossible to get infected by someone who is not close to you.

If these thoughts are troubling, don't worry! There is hope and there are ways to improve 3G skills. However, in our electronically isolated modern lifestyles, we must intentionally build spaces for values transmission, telling stories and experiencing life together. These teachable moments don't happen as naturally as in former times. A twenty-first century leader has to be more proactive than his or her counterpart even two decades ago.

Can it be done? Consider this up-to-date personal testimony on how a "Type A" leader made time for teachable moments in his family.

> Carl: We always tried to involve our two children in our work and ministry. This was good. It was "our thing" as a family.

> I have a strong work ethic and used to brag about never taking a vacation. I didn't realize the potential negative impact this was having on our family. My work was important and they just had to live with that. But after talking to you (the author) and others, we realized that the kids also needed to be part of our thing outside of our work life where we could focus on them as individuals and us as a family. We started doing family vacations.

> When we began, we didn't have much money. We tried to figure out what we could do that was fun and would make everybody want to come. We decided to go camping.

> I hate camping! My wife loves it! We packed up the car, refrigerator and all, because if I'm gonna go camping, at least we'll have cold drinks! We drove a thousand kilometers (600 miles) to a campsite next to an amusement park and camped for three whole days. I look back and say, "It was only three days!" But none of us will ever forget that first vacation.

> Though our son is not very sentimental or feeling-oriented, that special vacation time every

year has become of utmost importance. He is pretty adamant about not letting anybody else be with us. Even with his own friends, he's like, "Nope! This is just our time."

We keep the phones and computer turned off as much as we can. For our kids, that says a lot because they understand that I am driven and passionately want to see things move forward. So, for them to see that I am willing to stop everything, even just for three days or a week, speaks a lot about their value to us.

One wintertime, we were traveling through the States. A relative of mine looked at the bald tires on our borrowed car and said, "A blizzard is coming in. You need new tires." We did, but we had limited funds. It was a choice between new tires or going skiing. So, I did what any responsible father would do. We went skiing and had a blast! We made another memory for our family.

Sure enough, two of the four tires blew and had to be replaced. My kids love that story, because it helps them realize how important they are. People may say, "But that was irresponsible! What if you had an accident? That was a terrible decision!" Yep! It could have been a terrible decision. But prioritizing recreation times together is a strong value for us now.

I wouldn't recommend Carl's tire solution to everyone, but

you get the idea!

We've had a quick look at 3G basics. Now let's begin unpacking how it works in real time.

* * * * * * * * * *

questions for reflection:

- *Which kind of instruction is most natural for you: teaching, training or discipleship? Why?*

- *On the following 1 G- 3G scale, put an X where you feel your current lifestyle tends to be:*

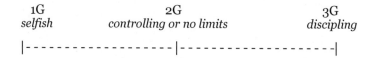

1G	2G	3G
selfish	*controlling or no limits*	*discipling*

|- - - - - - - - - - - - - - - - - - -|- - - - - - - - - - - - - - - - - - - -|

- *What do you think will be required to move your mark progressively toward a 3G lifestyle?*

chapter four endnotes

---

[23] Read the story in 1 Kings 12.

[24] *How to Be Jesus' Disciple: A Vision for Discipleship. http://www.focusequip.org/assets/pdf/how-to-discipleship-vision-preview.pdf*

[25] Matthew 11:29

[26] 1 Corinthians 11:1

[27] Matthew 13:1-23

[28] Mark 9:33-37

[29] Mark 10:14

How Does It Work?

That they should teach them to their children...
That they may arise and tell them to their
children.

-Psalm 78:5-6

Living a 3G lifestyle is not so much about the "what" as the "how." Your particular set of values is probably different from mine. Each of us has inherited something from our parents and added our own hard-won convictions—values tested by the fire of experience—into the package. This mix of old and new, inheritance and experience, defines the character of your family, business or organization. These are the things you truly believe and hope to instill in your employees or children. This is the "what" that each of us possesses and can pass on to the next generation.

Some values are based on negative reaction: "I will never abandon my kids like my father abandoned me!" or, "I will build a team rather than be a dictator like my former boss!" Others come from positive observation: "I will be a generous person like my mom," or, "Honesty is the best policy."

Values Versus Aspirations: Honest Abe?

We should note here the difference between a value and an aspiration. A value is something integrated into our lifestyle, a compass point that guides our daily decisions and reactions. An aspiration is something we would like to do. We're working on it, but it's not yet part of how we live. Aspirations can be taught, but they're often rejected when listeners see the teacher's behavior is different from their instruction. Values, on the other hand, are transmitted. What we are, in open and in secret, is what the next generation will catch and carry. "What they see is what they get."

> Values are transmitted…"What they see is what they get."

We observed in chapter two how Abraham was able to transmit a rock-solid faith through three generations. I'm sure he also would have liked to pass on honesty to his kids. That's certainly a good value.

Yet Genesis 20 records an incident revealing that honesty was more an aspiration than a value for Father Abraham.[30] Abe had an apparently drop-dead gorgeous wife named Sarah. While traveling through a place called Gerar, he faced a difficult decision. King Abimelech, the ruler of that area, customarily chose the most beautiful women of the land to join his harem. If she happened to be married, no problem. The husband was conveniently killed, and the suddenly single woman received a royal invitation.

Faced with a life-or-death crisis, truth became flexible for Abraham. "Say that you are my sister," he instructed Sarah. Sure enough, she was taken into royal custody. Fortunately, before the king could touch her, God intervened.[31] Abraham's aspiration was one thing; his demonstrated value was another.

Six chapters later, his son Isaac journeyed through the same land of Gerar, under the very same watchful gaze of "Abimelech."[32] Read what happens next:

> *When the men of the place asked about his wife, [Isaac] said, "She is my sister," for he was afraid to say, "my wife," thinking, "the men of the place might kill me on account of Rebekah, for she is beautiful." Genesis 26:7*

Déjà vu! Same place, same circumstances, same result. Like father like son! The apple didn't fall far from the tree. In Spanish we say, *de tal palo tal astilla:* "As is the stick, so is the splinter."

Aspirations are taught, values are caught. Abraham may have taught his sons about honesty. Isaac may have understood the value of keeping his word, but when push came to shove, he resorted to bending the truth, just like his dad! Abraham passed some good, some bad and some ugly values onto his succeeding generations. Perhaps his kids heard many soaring moral lessons, but the things that stuck were the episodes they lived together, actions observed and stories told.

Aspirations are taught, values are caught.

So if even towering moral giants like Abraham and Samuel didn't get it right, how can we ever pass on perfect values to succeeding generations?" *That's just the point; we can't!*

Perfection, unfortunately, remains outside the realm of human existence. Even if you were flawless, human nature resists duplication. The copies will always have defects.

Why? Because we are humans and not merely instinctual

animals. We have been endowed with free will, made "in the image of God." We have the ability to love, to create and also to make really stupid decisions. Neither we nor our sons and daughters were designed to be robots programmed to function exactly as programmed. If you hope by reading this book to turn out three generations of perfect children, carbon-copy co-wprkers, or duplicate disciples, forget it! It's not going to happen!

We will all leave some kind of legacy, guaranteed. We can attempt to control the behavior of our posterity (2G strategy) and it may work for as long as we are in control! The moment we're gone, however, history demonstrates that all our restraints and instruction will be cast off like rusty chains. People held captive against their will always look for escape.

****

CHECKPOINT: Some readers at this point may be hearing an inner voice shouting, "This 3G stuff may be good for others but not for me!"

Perhaps you have adult children, or you're an adult son or daughter who somehow missed out on the values transmission process. As a leader, maybe your followers have rejected you and your teaching or you just don't feel like you have much to pass on to another generation. Don't give up hope or put this book down just yet. You're not alone!

I encourage you to check out the testimonies of discouraged leaders, and fathers and mothers of prodigal sons and daughters, in the new and revised chapter twelve of this book. Their experience may be just the encouragement you need. There are second, third and fourth opportunities. There's still time and place to be a 3G leader or parent!

****

Our strategy must evolve from "chains" to "wings." We must purposely move away from a tendency to control towards a tendency to release, from condemnation to inspiration.

Our strategy must evolve from chains to wings.

It can be done whether you are married or single, in charge of a large network of employees or students, or have only one person who looks to you for influence. You can develop a 3G mentality and pursue a more intentional transmission of the values you hold dear.

There is a divine template for how to make this hand-off. Let's look at that key passage in Deuteronomy one more time:

> *These words, which I am commanding you today, shall be on your heart. You shall teach them diligently to your sons and shall talk of them when you sit in your house and when you walk by the way and when you lie down and when you rise up. You shall bind them as a sign on your hand and they shall be as frontals on your forehead. You shall write them on the doorposts of your house and on your gates. (Deuteronomy 6:6-8)*

The Israelites were instructed to repeat and relive the principles that God Himself had taught them. They were to do it in the morning, in the evening, when they went out, when they came home. These divinely dictated axioms were to be inscribed on the timbers of their houses and carried around personally. This is the essence of 3G: experience life together, evaluate on the basis of time-tested principles, release.

We can never control the outcome of our succeeding

generations, but we can follow the heavenly mandate, understand how values are caught, and alter our ways of doing things to maximize "catchable" values.

Let's look now at some real-life examples of 3G in action.

How to live 3G in the family.

Let's suppose you are a parent and your aspiration is to see your children develop healthy families of their own. What does a 1G lifestyle look like? This one is pretty easy.

1G: Live only for yourself, have a moral failure, spend zero time with the family.

Not much comment needed. Pretty good recipe for disaster. Remember, 1G can also characterize the lifestyle of a selfless individual, always serving others but neglecting times "along the way" with those closest to him or her.

How, then, would we portray a 2G lifestyle?

2G: Control all family decisions. Protect them from contact with undesirable elements. Filter all their friendships (and monitor their social network accounts!)

This parent may have good intentions. He/she may or may not be morally upright. However, by controlling all aspects of their children's decisions, they are choking off creativity and limiting important experiences. They may control the home environment but they will fail to successfully transmit values to the next generation. Conversely, letting them make all decisions can also be 2G! No limits and no guidelines produce insecurity and even dangerous situations. If you don't set limits or boundaries, your children's freedom will be offset by a distorted view of authority. You may set an inspiring example when present, but once you're gone, they won't have the resources or experience to follow that example.

What about 3G?

3G: Give them increasing areas of responsibility in the home. Let them share in some major family decision. Base discipline decisions on values, not on how mad you feel. Give them choices as much as possible.

Remember, a 3G lifestyle is focused on *release*, not on *control*. Let's examine these descriptions of a 3G strategy by sharing a few accidental discoveries from our own family's storyline.

> Remember, a 3G lifestyle is focused on *release*, not on *control*.

Give Them Increasing Responsibility

My wife is a pro in this area. If you entered our kitchen today, you would probably not find plates to set the table. Years ago, when our children were young, Patti decided to put all the dishes and serving items on the lowest shelves. Why? So that even our three-year-old could help with dinner preparation.

Sure, we broke a few plates and glasses in the process, but our kids learned at a very young age that they could be a responsible part of our family meals. I'm not so good at this.

My mom taught me how to iron shirts and somehow made it fun. Not one of my four children nor my wife likes to iron. I offered to pay for each shirt, set up the ironing board in front of the TV, but nothing worked. I'm like the guy who complains to his wife, "I'm probably the only businessman in town who irons his own shirts on Monday morning," to which she replies, "That's because all the others ironed theirs on Sunday night!" I'm a 3G failure when it comes to ironing shirts! But we were more successful with doing laundry.

We'll never forget one particular King's Kids tour when all the older teenager guys approached us with a desperate request. "Can you please move Eduardo[33] to a different room?" They were all packed into one small classroom, sleeping on the floor of a church. We asked the reason for the transfer request. "Because...well...he smells bad!" they finally revealed.

"Guys' rooms always smell bad," I responded, not wanting them to miss the valuable lessons of teamwork and a little suffering for the common good.

"No," they insisted, "this is baaaaaad! We don't think he's ever washed his socks in his entire life! You gotta help us!"

We took some other leaders, opened the door, and the odor hit us like a loaded tractor-trailer at freeway speed. It was baaaaaad! Pinching our noses, we answered in a nasalized voice, "Ngo kay. Ngui gwill snee ngwat ngui can ndo." But how were we going to overcome this reeking reality?

1Gers would say something like, "Let them worry about it. It's not our problem." 2Gers might punish the offender, remove him to another place or even secretly wash the socks and underwear. Anything to solve the problem, reduce the tension and sweep the embarrassment under the rug.

Patti bravely volunteered what we would now call a 3G approach. She filled up a plastic baby pool in the middle of the church patio and invited eleven-year-old Eduardo to a private one-on-one session. "Eduardo, has anyone ever taught you how to wash clothes by hand?"

When he replied negatively, Patti, without referring to any

complaints, showed him the basics: apply detergent, thrash in the water, rub dirty parts together, more thrashing, squeeze, rinse and hang. "Now, you do it," she offered.

After the second or third set of socks hung limply on an improvised clothesline, Eduardo's face beamed. "I can do this! This is cool!" He scampered off, a confident smile brightening his puckish face.

The story didn't end there. Later we heard that Eduardo went back to the guys' room and offered to wash everyone's socks. It became his way of making friends with the older ones and feeling accepted as part of the team. We didn't have to move Eduardo out of the room. The others wanted him close to keep washing their laundry!

Let Them Share in Some Family Decisions

Before moving to Spain, we Clewetts made a monthlong trip to "spy out the land." We knew this would be quite a shift, not only for us parents, but also for our children who were aged seven, six and two. Leaving friends, downsizing possessions, learning a new language and getting used to different foods—a tall order for anyone. Missionary colleagues warned us how important it was for our kids, even at an early age, to be "in" on this important decision. As we traversed the Iberian Peninsula, we made a special effort to stop at the beaches, check out a couple of amusement parks, and sample all the Spanish varieties of candy along the way, as well as visit collaborators and churches, doing the adult tasks that tend to be pretty boring for kids.

When we returned to the States and asked, "Who wants to move to Spain?" we got a unanimous yes from all parties! I know, I know! That's more like a bribe than a proper parenting technique. All the same, it worked and the principle is valid.

My son, Kenny, says, "This (sharing in that decision process) was one of the shaping moments of my life and the thing that saved us from hating Spain during the first few months." And what if they all had said no? I trust we parents would have reconsidered or at least waited until there was a consensus.

Let your kids in on important family decisions as much as you can. James C. Hunter, in his remarkable book about servant-leadership, notes, "Being in on things always rates higher than money in surveys of employee satisfaction."[34] Of course, much depends on the age and maturity of the child or employee you're dealing with. Yet the effect is the same. Whether it's choosing the color of the new car, voting on the design of the new logo, or deciding what to name the dog, if your second generation helps choose, they share ownership of the decision.

Base Discipline on Values, Not on How Mad You Feel

Dale Kauffman, the founder of King's Kids, tells the story of an unforgettable Sunday morning. Decked out in his favorite suit, Dale was adding finishing touches to a sermon with head buried in his Bible and study notes. He didn't see his young son waddling into the living room balancing a tray stacked high with pancakes slathered in syrup and a huge glass of purple grape juice. "Daddy, a surprise for you!" his son said, smiling as wide as his cherubic face would allow. Dale looked up just in time to see his youngster trip on the carpet, launching him and a breakfast fit for a king squarely onto Dad's lap. His first reflex, and probably most us would do about the same, was to let his toddler have it. This was his best suit, these were stains that probably would never come out. How could he be so clumsy? Didn't he understand that food should never be brought into the living room?

Surveying the damage, however, he saw a young son trembling in terror and confusion. "I'm so sorry, Daddy! I didn't mean it."

A 1G reaction could be: "Go away! You've done enough damage already!" A 2G response: "You can't pay to replace this suit, but you can certainly clean up this mess. Now get moving!" Fortunately, as tears began to well up in those innocent eyes, compassion overcame anger. Dale reached out and just hugged the shaking little boy and held on.

"Thank you so much for preparing that breakfast for me. I really appreciate it and am so sorry I didn't get to enjoy it! You are so much more important than this suit. I can replace clothes but I can never replace you!"

Can you feel the value of unconditional love being pressed into the wet cement of that child's heart?

It's so hard but so important that we pause before reacting to the mistakes our followers, employees, students and children make. So often, just asking yourself the question, "What principle is in play here?" or, "How can we react to this problem in a way that seals a permanent value into their memory bank?" works so much better than controlling or dismissing the problem. We can turn a nasty situation into a teachable moment. It's not always easy but it is 3G.

> It's so hard but so important that we pause before reacting to the mistakes our followers and children make.

Give Choices As Much As Possible

When people are allowed to choose, either reaping the rewards of good choices or suffering the consequences of bad ones, they begin to take responsibility for their actions and they mature. A 3G leadership style tends toward setting boundaries and giving choices as opposed to dictating behavior and threatening punishment.

My intent in this book, again, is not to write a complete manual on parenting or leadership. There are many great books that explore ideas of boundaries and consequences in depth far beyond the constraints of space or the authority of this writer. A few sterling examples from my favorite authors are listed in endnotes of this chapter.[35] But here's one more story to illustrate this important principle.

Like many parents of young children, we were struggling at bedtime with our then-four-year-old son, Kenny. Once placed under the covers by his loving parents, he recited a dizzying list of reasons to get back up. He needed to go to the bathroom, his teeth required brushing, we didn't read him the right story, the hall light was too bright, his throat was sore. Anyone who has been a parent (or a kid) knows how this endurance test works. Eventually, all these vital excuses tend to wear down even the most authoritarian parental heart. As Kenny wailed down the hallway demanding his rights to get up for yet another uncompleted task, my wife, Patti, surrendered.

"Curtis, can you please do something?"

Having been a kid myself, I knew what was going on. My favorite excuse used to be, "I have a canker sore," requiring a trip to the kitchen for a dab of baking soda to relieve the pain. To be truthful, I didn't even know what a canker sore was, but if it resulted in extra stay-up time, why not?

I ambled down the hall to our son's room. "Kenny, it's time for sleep," I cajoled in my most fatherly, reassuring voice, Suddenly a deafening and carefully timed "Waaaaaaaaaah!" cut off all further adult reasoning. Okay, it was time for action! I was ready to threaten food rationing, a wooden spoon to the posterior, anything to get this kid to shut up and allow his loving parents to get some sleep. However, I had heard about this boundary-and-choices idea and decided to give it a shot.

My mind raced to invent a binary set of choices with clear consequences. Between wailings he demanded that we leave the door more open. "Kenny," I said, "here's the deal. I will leave your door open a crack if you stop crying"—interrupted by an even louder howl—"and if you don't stop crying, the door will be closed. Got it?" The tantrum ramped up another notch. Game on! "Okay, it's your choice," I said as I shut the door. Wow, I didn't know human lungs were capable of the decibel range now assaulting our home.

After enduring two full minutes of auditory pain, during a lung-filling pause before the next outcry, I cracked open the door and asked if he was ready to stop. More yelling, this time coupled with accusations of abuse and threats to sue me, if I remember right! Door closed for two more minutes. The second time I opened the door, something unprecedented happened—he quieted down! He was ready to negotiate.

"Can you leave the door open just a crack?"

"If you stop crying."

"Just a crack, okay?"

"No more crying?"

"Okay."

And that was it. I was in shock! We were going to get a full night's sleep and my wife thought I was a rock star!

Not all parenting battles end so well. Sometimes we are just too busy, it's an emergency, we're out in public, or we're just too mad to think through options and consequences. But they do work, and Kenny began to take more responsibility for his bedtime routine.

Set limits, provide clear choices with well-defined and agreed-to consequences, and let them choose. Then, stick to your guns! Let the consequences have their effect. You're giving them a chance to develop their own values. It works in the family, it works with employees, it works in educational settings. Quick thinking and practice are required, but these are 3G approaches that work with all ages in most situations.

Set limits, provide clear choices with agreed-to consequences, and let them choose. You're giving them a chance to develop values.

* * * * * * * * * * *

questions for reflection:

- *Think of some recent choices you made as decision maker over your family or team. How did your children or team members react? How could they have been more involved making the choice and gaining ownership over the decision?*

- *What are two or three tasks you do now that could easily be done by your second generation even if not quite as well as you?*

- *What will it cost, in terms of time or lesser quality of the result, if you were to delegate and train them in these tasks? Is it worth it?*

chapter five endnotes

[30] *Genesis 20:1-14*

[31] *Genesis 26:6-10*

[32] Probably a son of former king with same honorific name like "Ceasar" or "Pharaoh."

[33] Name changed in case the guilty party ever reads this.

[34] James C. Hunter, *The Servant,* p 43-44

[35] *Parenting:*
Dobson, James C. *The New Dare to Discipline"(1996).*
Cloud, Henry and Townsend, John. *Boundaries with Kids: When to Say Yes, When to Say No, to Help Your Children Gain Control of Their Lives (2001).*

Leadership:
Hunter, James C. *"The Servant: (1998).*
Cloud, Henry. *"Boundaries for Leaders: Results, Relationships and Being Ridiculously in Charge" (2013).*

CHAPTER SIX

3G Applied

*The true meaning of life is to plant trees under
whose shade you do not expect to sit.*

-Nelson Henderson
19th Century American settler

Let's stop for a moment and take stock of some of the key
points we have covered so far:

- **A 3G lifestyle seeks to transmit values through a
second generation to influence at least a third
generation.**

- **A 3G strategy provides space to experience life
together and makes time for evaluation, linking
principles and values to what was experienced.**

- **3G is characterized by giving out responsibility as
early as possible.**

- **3G embraces "discipleship," "learning along the
way" and "teachable moments"** as key channels of
value transmission.

- **3G is focused more on *releasing* than *controlling***
  the next generation. Questions work better than dictates in
  most situations.

Now let's put this to work in some values that I assume
most people would like to transmit well.

Is there any reader who purposely wants their children or
co-workers to be sexually immoral, or irresponsible with time
or money? I didn't think so! How do we instill healthy
attitudes in these areas, especially if we were not, perhaps, the
most shining example of moral uprightness or responsibility in
our own youth? Good question!

Let's apply our 1G, 2G, 3G paradigm and then explore how
that might work in typical settings in families and leadership
teams.

Morality in the Family

1G: Live a promiscuous lifestyle yourself, but make sex a taboo
subject at home. Expect kids to learn all they need to know in
school. Never let on that you and your spouse do have sex and
that it's a good thing.

2G: Forbid the next generation from any contact with the
opposite sex, or set no boundaries at all! Talk about sex
ambiguously, make off-color jokes or dehumanize the act. Lie
about your own first sexual experiences if they were not in line
with your current convictions.

3G: Rather than forbid your kids to go to their friends' place,
invite friends over to your house (especially during vital older
childhood/preteen years) to observe how they get along.

Engage in conversation about things you see together that do not match your values. Talk honestly, in private and at the age-appropriate moment, about your own mistakes and wise choices with the opposite sex. Help them to set boundaries. Be a sounding board without condemnation in their moments of confusion or curiosity.

I don't think anyone gets this gradual and healthy introduction to sex education perfect. However, 1G and 2G strategies often produce confused and fragile offspring, easy prey to the anywhere-anytime porn on their personal electronic devices. It used to be that parents planned to discuss the "birds and the bees" in the preteen years (ten to twelve years old). Not anymore. To seriously help your child form values, experts advise starting at age seven or eight or even younger! I have placed in the endnotes some Internet resources, both Christian and non, about how to have "the talk" if you are at this stage in your family or group.[36]

So how do we go beyond controlling our kids' access to sexual material to help them establish their own healthy values?

Our oldest daughter, Kari, is a licensed psychologist and family therapist. She often reminds me of a particular 3G moment that occurred during our family's first years in Europe. When we arrived in the early '90s, Spain was a bit more relaxed than America in their sexual mores. All the beaches were topless, and nude media was visible in every corner kiosk. There were no opaque rack inserts hiding the magazine covers like at US convenience stores. Movies with R and X ratings regularly invaded our TV screens during daytime hours.

I quickly discovered that a 2G "defensive" strategy to restrict our kids' exposure to porn and its negative consequences was just not going to work. We needed a different plan. When we talk about 3G and "experiencing things together," of course there are limits when it comes to the subject of sex! What to do?

Once, in Kari's early teen years, a rather inappropriate love scene was unfolding on our TV set. Our kids had selected the channel. In earlier years, we would clear our throats out loud, and if that didn't work, we would get up and change the channel or fast-forward the video (we're talking the '90s here!) to indicate disapproval and a "you should know better" kind of parental attitude. This time we were silent as clothes came off and steam was rising. At the commercial break, I apparently asked something like, "So, what did you think about that last scene?"

"Oh, Dad!" came the exasperated reply.

"I mean, the guy and the gal weren't married, were they?" I ventured.

"No, probably not," Kari countered.

"You guys have some friends whose parents are unmarried or divorced. How do you think that affects their home life?"

According to Kari, it opened up an interesting conversation, connecting the dots between illicit affairs and the resulting damage to the family. The next time a racy scene came on, our older kids knew what was coming and sighed when I made another attempt to talk about the values in play.

Kari likes to say that after that particular episode, whenever something sleazy graced the video screen, she had an uncontrollable urge to get up and change the channel, dreading that long awkward conversation afterward, even if her parents weren't around. Something 3G took place right in front of our TV set and we didn't even know it!

Let's evaluate briefly what happened in terms of our 3G principles stated at the beginning of this chapter:

1. **A 3G lifestyle seeks to transmit values through a second generation to influence at least a third generation.** Through this experience and many others, Kari captured a set of values that she now teaches as a professional psychologist and practices as a role model for many others. That awkward moment is now an anecdote that is influencing others who attend her seminars and read her material.

2. **A 3G strategy provides space to experience life together.** I have to admit, watching TV was not necessarily an "intentionally provided space to experience life together" with our children. However, Patti and I did take time to sit with them and watch their programming on occasion. It was vital that we didn't miss these "teachable moments" because we were too busy to ever have downtime with our children.

3. **3G is characterized by giving out responsibility as early as possible.** When our kids were younger, we did restrict their viewing material. But this time, we didn't change the channel. Our second generation became responsible for what programming they would watch. Yet they were also accountable by means of after-conversations, helping them filter and judge content according to their emerging value system.

4. **3G embraces "discipleship," "learning along the way" and "teachable moments."** As parents or teachers, we may think that seminars and classroom sessions are the best way to teach morality. We would be mistaken. Don't get me wrong here. Clear, carefully prepared teaching is a vital and important underpinning to help young people make good moral decisions. However, often these unguarded but "teachable" moments, conversations where values are linked to experience, will seal those values into place.

5. **3G is focused more on *releasing* than *controlling*; questions work better than dictates in most situations.** Even if we didn't plan the setting, we did take a moment to evaluate the awkward experience, using open questions ("What did you think about that?") versus closed dictates ("You are forbidden to watch TV ever again without parents in the room!"). It was not easy to restrain our hands from turning the TV dials, but we knew that controlling and "defensive" strategies wouldn't work in this instance. Kari says she learned how to "reflect and process what I watched, deciding if I wanted to agree with the values portrayed, change the channel, or disagree and continue watching while knowing I was acting against my own conscience." Learning to make her own informed choices helped Kari establish values that would become uniquely hers. She gained confidence and now has convictions that can be shared with others she influences– our third generation!

Time Responsibility in a Leadership Team

1G: Set rules for others that you never follow. Arrive two hours late without comment but shame others who dare enter the office five minutes after the appointed time.

2G: Always be punctual but never approach other members of the team about their tardiness. Assume they will somehow conform to your standard.

3G: Set a good example. Publicly and privately acknowledge staff people who made sacrifices to arrive on time. Set up private meetings with time-challenged team members to explore the issue and determine together positive steps to solve the problem.

Anyone who has led teams or dealt with employees recognizes this problem! In mixed cultural settings, this can become quite a difficult issue. I live in Southern Europe on the Mediterranean Coast—what sociologists would consider a "warm climate" culture—that is more driven by events than schedule. In Spain, if you arrive five to fifteen minutes past an appointed start time, that's not necessarily considered late. In even warmer climes such as West Africa, where our middle daughter, Kindra, lives, several hours or even an entire day late is acceptable. Compare that with my German or Swiss friends who consider two minutes tardy unacceptable, and you get the idea.

If you are in a business that must deliver its product or service on time, or in a group staging public events that will start at a certain hour: how do you get everyone on the same schedule? How do you allow for creativity, make room for different cultures, and still get the job delivered on time?

Ha! If someone has the complete answer to that one let me know! My own success has been varied over the years. However, we can propose some 3G approaches that will move your team in the right direction.

First of all, you must be a good example. Nothing creates more resentment than a "do-as-I-say-not-as-I-do" attitude on the part of a leader or boss.

2G leaders stop there and hope for the best. "I got here on time. Why can't you?" How does a 3G leader deal with the chronically late co-worker?

Obvious but very important: they set up a *private* meeting to deal with the issue. Perhaps there are others who also need time management instruction, but when we call out and put down people in public, we resort to shame, not inspiration. Shame tends to break down and harden. Inspiration builds up and softens. Which one do you think works better?

Shame tends to break down and harden. Inspiration builds up and softens. Which one do you think works better?

In the meeting, use *The Formula*. I don't remember where I learned this particular way of dealing with conflicts, but it has saved me many a painful experience when approaching issues like this. It's 3G and it works!

The Formula treats a problem objectively rather than subjectively. Instead of beginning with accusation: "You did this! What do you have to say for yourself?" you attempt to put the problem on the table where it can be examined by both parties. You separate the issue from the person, consider the consequences and together determine steps to resolve the problem. You're asking them to explore the values in play and calling on them to take part in the resolution.

The Formula for Resolving Conflicts

1. **Determine together exactly what happened.**

2. **Tell the other person how that action made you and/or others feel.**

3. **Ask them to comment on the incident.**

4. **Determine together appropriate steps to solve the problem.**

5. **(Optional) Set an evaluation time in the near future to measure progress.**

Let's suppose that Bob, a capable graphic artist, just can't seem to get to your team meetings or deliver his work on time. There's always an excuse: the computer broke down, he had to take his child to an after-school program, he didn't understand the meeting time, and so on. You have tried the usual tricks and subtle encouragements: telling him how important his work is, giving him a small pay incentive for early arrival, offering to pick him up on the way to the meeting. Nothing works. He regularly comes in twenty minutes late. What do you do?

First, always wait for a specific incident. It is nearly impossible to refer to a bad attitude or habit when resolving a conflict. You need to name a specific example so both of you can make sure you are referring to the same exact circumstances. Conflicts get nastier when people feel falsely accused or misunderstood. Here's an example.

Today, Friday, the team meeting was scheduled for 6 p.m. You know Bob received notice by email and at least two separate electronic messages. Also, he was there last week when the next meeting was announced. Sure enough, Bob comes through the door at 6:21. You ask him to stay on after the meeting is over. He's a little nervous, knowing something is up. Let's see what *The Formula* looks like in action.

1. Determine together exactly what happened.

Begin politely. "Bob, thanks for staying after the meeting. I trust you and your family are well?"

"Yeah, yeah, we're doing all right," he replies, eyes darting around the room for clues of what might come next.

"Bob, I want to talk to you about our team meeting today."

"Okay."

"I want to make sure that you were aware of the starting time of the meeting. Did you get the email notice sent out on Wednesday and the staff bulletin sent out on Thursday announcing the meeting time?"

"Uh, yeah. I think so."

"Okay, and today as you came in, I glanced up at the clock and noticed it was 6:21, does that sound about right?

"Actually it was only 6:15 by my watch," Bob counters, knowing the hammer is about to fall.

"Okay, 6:15. So you arrived fifteen minutes later than the appointed meeting time, is that right?"

"Yeah, I suppose so."

Now, here at this moment is where you can choose a 2G accusatory approach or you go for 3G. It's so easy to become the district attorney, making the defendant squirm in the witness chair and continue the interrogation. "So explain yourself! This is the fifth time this month. Come on, Bob, get your act together!" Can you feel the anger and shame rising in Bob as he tries to react to being blindsided? A 2G blame game might get Bob temporarily back in line, but it will unlikely build a personal value of punctuality in his life. If you're his boss, get ready soon to deal with either this same issue or another one born of resentment at how this one was treated.

Let's see how *The Formula* would continue this conversation. You have set the incident on the table. Now both of you can examine the issue and its consequences.

1. **Tell the other person how that action made you and/or others feel.**

"Bob, I need to tell you something. I'm so proud of the wonderfully creative work that you do. It has been very well received by our clients and our community. I recruited you because I saw someone who could add so much value to our team. (It never hurts to start with affirmation!)

"Yet, when you are late, it affects both me and team. We all have crammed schedules. Everyone works hard to come to these meetings on time so we can maximize our creative juices, solve problems and really bond as a team. When one member is late, we all suffer a little. Team members start asking, 'Why should I sacrifice time with my family to be punctual if we don't start on schedule?'

"I'm unable to conduct an effective meeting because we have to go over things twice to include those arriving late. In short, it makes me feel weak and a little frustrated as a leader and hurts our team."

By referring to how you feel, you are pointing the finger back to yourself. The incident made you feel _____. Feelings are not good or bad. They just happen, sometimes provoked by circumstances, sometimes for no reason at all. Describing the emotion and laying it on the table gives you both a chance to look at it without justifying, defending or accusing the other.

2. **Ask them to comment about the incident.**

"Can you comment about what happened today?"

You can start with, "I'm sure you didn't mean to cause hardship" or something similar, but you must give the other person a moment to describe their side of the story, once the details of the incident (he arrived late) have been agreed upon.

"Well, I was working on the latest project, you know. Wanted to get it just right and I just lost track of the time. I'm sorry, it won't happen again."

"Bob, I appreciate your extra efforts. I really do. But it does not change the damage that late arrival causes to me and the team." (Notice language about the damage "it" causes to the team, not the damage "he" is causing to the team. Stay objective. It's the behavior we are talking about, not the person!)

3. **Determine together appropriate steps to solve the problem.**

"How can we, together, make sure it doesn't happen again?"

"Uh, I don't know. It's kinda been a problem I've had since early childhood."

Notice that this approach permits both you and Bob to explore the possible causes. You are not accusing Bob of being lazy or irresponsible. Bob does not have to activate his defense-missile batteries against your attack on his character. Both of you, together, are looking for solutions. This process may or may not lead to the root causes of the problem. That's not always your concern if you're his work boss. If you are his mentor, this objective approach may well open a channel for talking about character issues.

"Well, think of something within your ability that you could do to make sure you are here on time and can be a support to the team."

"Hmmm, what if I put the meeting date on my smartphone calendar and set up a fifteen-minute advance alarm?"

"That's a good idea! Do you think it will work?"

He is engaged in a positive pursuit of solution rather than denying responsibility and deflecting blame. When you both can agree on action steps, then it may be appropriate to set a time, maybe one or two weeks later, to get together again and see how he is doing. For some people, this is vital. It shows that they are important to you. They also will have the chance to either feel encouraged by their progress or to understand how chronic the problem really is. And, you are addressing the issue together. Bob is finally able to connect the dots and see why other team members treat him so brusquely when they meet. He is squaring off against an objective goal—to get there on time—and you are going deeper than just demanding punctuality. You're helping Bob to develop responsibility in a determined area of his life and understand why it is important. You're becoming a 3G problem solver.

* * * * * * * * * * *

questions for reflection

- *What was the essence of your first "sex talk"? Who did you hear it from? What would have made it better or more effective for you?*

- *Think back to a recent conflict or one that is happening now. Imagine you are now with that person in conversation and go through the steps of* The Formula. *Even write down your statements and their likely responses.*

chapter six endnotes

---

[36] *The Birds and the Bees: Talking to Your Kids About Sex Comments.* https://powertochange.com/family/talkkids/

Mary VanCley. *How to Talk to Your Child About Sex (ages 6 to 8). http:// www.babycenter.com/0_how-to-talk-to-your-child-about-sex-ages-6-to-8_67908.bc*

https://consumer.healthday.com/encyclopedia/children-s-health-10/child-development-news-124/how-to-talk-to-your-child-about-sex-ages-6-to-12-645918.html

The Lion and the Bear

The LORD who delivered me from the paw of the lion and from the paw of the bear, He will deliver me from the hand of this Philistine.

-*David*

Most of us know a bit about the story of David facing off with the giant Goliath, an incredible feat of youthful courage and valor. Where did he get this invincible attitude? Careful reading of the Old Testament Scriptures reveal that David had already faced bigger and more fearsome enemies in his "even younger" youth. Listen to this exchange between David and King Saul:

> *Then Saul said to David, "You are not able to go against this Philistine to fight with him; for you are but a youth while he has been a warrior from his youth." But David said to Saul, "Your servant was tending his father's sheep. When a lion or a bear came and took a lamb from the flock, I went out after him and attacked him, and rescued it from his mouth; and when he rose up against me, I seized him by his beard and struck*

*him and killed him..." And David said, "The
LORD who delivered me from the paw of the lion
and from the paw of the bear, He will deliver me
from the hand of this Philistine." And Saul said to
David, "Go, and may the LORD be with you." (1
Samuel 17:33-37)*

David may have been young when he volunteered to fight
Goliath, but he was not a novice! Through the cold nights and
burning heat of the Judaean wilderness, his fighting skills had
been honed, his spirit steeled. Yet he was armed with only a
leather sling and five smooth stones while the Philistine giant
carried an arsenal and was protected by body armor and a
bronze helmet.

The battle was indeed lopsided. But, surprise! Goliath was
the disadvantaged one!

According to ancient war experts, a skilled slinger could
hurtle rocks accurately at an impact effectiveness greater than
a .357 magnum bullet at the muzzle![37] In fact, "Goliath had
just as much of a chance against David as any Bronze Age
warrior with a sword would have had against an adolescent
armed with an automatic pistol."[38]

Goliath was no match for the young Israelite who had
already taken down a lion and a bear and was now armed with
advanced weaponry. It was a battle tilted heavily in David's
favor!

In our particular set of values in King's Kids, International,
we call this the "lion and the bear principle." People faced with
challenges early in life—the lion and the bear in David's
example—are better prepared for greater challenges awaiting
them in the future. If our children and followers are going to
take on the "giants" of their generation, they need to be
exposed to a few lions and bears in their early years.

Let's take a crack at applying this to developing financial responsibility in our 2nd generation.

Starting Early with Finances

Considering how to pass on healthy financial principles to our progeny, let's begin with our 1G, 2G and 3G paradigm:

1G: Never set a budget, spend everything you can, max out your credit cards and "live for today." Complain constantly about never being able to afford nice things.

2G: Create a good college trust fund and retirement plan. Make sure your kids always have money in their pockets, and rescue them immediately if they ever get into debt. Or, never talk about money and assume they will learn all they need to know "the hard way."

3G: Set up tasks children can do in the house to earn money for things they want. Teach them how to set a budget, and help them understand the value of charitable giving. Let them in on major family decisions: a new job, a move to a new place, a workplace dilemma, and so on.

I'm convinced that way too many young people enter adulthood with a poorly developed sense of financial prudence. They have either been pampered by well-meaning parents or else learned to scrimp on everything because, according to their parental example, they will never be able to afford a decent lifestyle.

Healthy work habits—arriving on time, respecting your boss, following tasks through to the end, meeting deadlines, pursuing excellence—are not being taught or learned very well in the homes of the 21st century. Partially as a result, we are experiencing a growing percentage of unemployable youth. In Spain we call them *ni-nis* (*ni trabajan, ni estudian*, "they don't work and they don't study"). They live at home well into their thirties and even forties. *Ni-nis* and their counterparts in other cultures are straining the social net of entire nations saddled with lower production and increasing entitlement expenses.

Can this trend be reversed? I believe so, but it must begin in that fully equipped 3G laboratory called the home.

At the risk of sounding nostalgic, I remember growing up in Sonoma, in the middle of Northern California wine country, and how my parents offered numerous ways for us Clewett kids to earn money and learn about financial management. They provided well and we never lacked basic necessities. But when it came to wants—extra money for soft drinks at the corner gas station, a whistle ring, firecrackers for 4th of July Independence Day—we had to earn it. We could pick blackberries for 25¢ a basket, move rocks for 50¢ an hour, wash the car for $1 and yes, even iron shirts for 20¢ each.

Nowadays, somebody would call those pitiful sums a violation of child labor laws (especially moving the rocks!) but we found it perfectly normal. We grew up learning: a) There was always a way to get some things we felt were vital to enjoy our youthful years, and b) Paying for these comforts would cost time, effort and even sweat. We had to put off temporary pleasure now—sitting around, playing football, catching salamanders and building dams in the nearby creek—in order to enjoy a greater pleasure later. (A cold Royal Crown cola on a hot summer day, it didn't get much better than that!)

Okay, that was nearly a half-century ago. What about now? Most families don't live in the idyllic countryside but in great urban areas with no lawn to mow or rocks to move. (Thank God!)

These ideas can be directly applied to other situations outside the home. Whenever we took young people on King's Kids outreaches, we always trained a couple of teenagers how to count money and set up a small ledger for daily expenses. We would teach them to organize coins and bills in piles and count them the way banks do. Then we'd work together squaring accounts or the checkbook. Even though an experienced adult could do the job in half the time, it wasn't about getting the job done fast, it was about transferring skills from older to younger. As an added bonus, many interesting conversations took place between the generations as we tidied coin stacks and tallied up expenses. We purposely invested in these restless teenagers eager to finish and get to the swimming pool. It took time and patience.

> It wasn't about getting the job done fast, it was about transferring skills from older to younger.

Yet I can think now of people like Miriam, who couldn't distinguish a debit from a credit, but who, a few years later, was cleaning up the accounting for an entire missionary base in Brazil. Or Mérie whose financial skills helped her get her first well-paying job in Barcelona. Or Eduardo (the boy with the dirty socks) who probably owns a laundromat someplace!

Providing opportunities at a young age to earn money in household chores is still not a bad way to begin. You may not have rocks and blackberries, but what about laundry, dishes, vacuuming, windows, ironing (good luck!), cooking, shopping, or data entry? The list is potentially endless for creative parents and leaders. Now some are already saying, "Well, shouldn't they do these things anyway without a monetary reward?"

I personally think that every child should have certain

chores they are taught to do routinely (that's easy to say but not always easy to do). There are other tasks that enter the realm of what Mom and Dad would normally do that can be taught and then given out as "extra credit" to children, earning points, privileges and even money.

IMPORTANT: Remember the case study of Eduardo in chapter five? Don't forget to take time to train step-by-step until the younger or more novice co-worker has mastered the task. This promotes confidence and motivation. Maybe offer something extra for a job particularly well done. You are investing in their future! It may take longer. The spot on the rug may not come all the way out. The composted juice from the organic garbage may have leaked a little on the floor. But is it worth it to see your child conquer his or her Goliath in the coming years? This is 3G talk!

> Don't forget to take time to train step-by-step until the younger protégé has mastered the task.

In the back of this book is a section called "Twenty-one 3G Ideas for Families and Leadership Teams," among which are a number of other suggestions for developing financial values in your second generation. Check them out and see if any are applicable to your family or group.

A Special Word for Parents of Preteens

Before going on, I would like to pass on one of the most helpful ideas we have come across to help preteens put "a lion and a bear" in their backpacks before entering the turbulent teenage years. The actual article, *Giant Steps* by Dave and Claudia Arp appeared in a 1994 parenting magazine, which, unfortunately, is now out of print.[39] Here is a brief description of this teenage rite of passage that both our children and we parents agree was a cool thing to do.

There's something special and mysterious about the age of thirteen. Puberty tends to strike on or near this milestone. The school system is no longer so tightly structured. In many cases, students are now allowed to take elective classes or go out for sports teams. Preteens are suddenly faced with making decisions and thinking about what career track they wish to pursue. Their world becomes scary as they compare themselves with other classmates and realize that they may not sing as well, be as popular or get similar grades for the same amount of work as their friends. Crossing the teenage boundary successfully can result in confident and adventurous adolescent years. Crossing it badly can cause misery and any number of complexes lasting well into adulthood. How can parents help?

The Arps suggested setting up a series of "challenges" on or near the child's twelfth birthday. The idea was to sit down together and devise tasks that would require more than a week of effort—something just beyond their current abilities. This would give them valuable experience in setting goals, putting off present pleasure for future reward, making small sacrifices, and believing "I can do this!" to take into their next few years. As an additional motivation, parents and child select together a thirteenth birthday present of the child's choice with almost the sky as the limit.

There were four categories of challenges: *spiritual, practical, physical* and *intellectual.* Each challenge had to be completed before their thirteenth birthday to validate the more-generous-than-usual birthday gift. Our oldest daughter, Kari, decided she wanted to take a trip back to the States from Spain, by herself, to visit friends and family she missed dearly. Patti and I cleared our throats a bit, analyzing the costs. "This is going to be an expensive lesson for us if it works!" The challenges we determined together were:

- **Spiritual challenge:** to establish a daily Bible-reading habit and read consecutively about half of the Bible from Genesis through the Psalms.

- **Practical challenge:** to play the classic Beethoven piano piece "Moonlight Sonata."

- **Physical challenge:** to complete a full aerial turn in her roller skating (she could already do a half-turn).

- **Intellectual challenge:** to read through another book about adolescence.

The results were impressive. I remember the look on her face when she finally completed that full flip in her skating program. She developed a love for and competency in music. Kari made it through the doldrums of Leviticus and Deuteronomy (going on later to an intensive biblical mastery course) and best of all, she was able to hit the ground running into adolescence. It didn't mean that her years of thirteen to nineteen were without conflict. However, it did give her and her siblings, when they completed their challenges, bedrock confidence and experience in setting goals and pursuing a vision.

Leadership guru Peter Drucker said:

> *Bind a young person to tasks that are easily within their ability and for the rest of their lives they will conform to mediocrity. Bind them with tasks that are just beyond their ability and they*

will continually search for excellence.[40]

Michael Valles, talking about wisely passing on a financial inheritance, likewise concludes:

Mediocrity should never be accepted...Excellence, however, needs to be taught and encouraged just as any other value. Doing your best should apply to everything that a young person does, not simply in those things that he or she enjoys.

Once young people have learned to give themselves to the task placed before them, they are then able to direct that "do your best" mentality to wherever it may be needed. This produces real character, and will enable them to focus on the best use of the assets under their control ... This will also reduce waste and extravagance.[41]

Organizing these challenges required extra time for us parents in planning, encouraging, reminding and monitoring their progress. Yet it was another opportunity to experience life together at this vital coming-of-age moment.

Do you have preteens or know someone who does? Try out this 3G activity. Your succeeding generations will thank you!

One final thought before closing this chapter:

3G leaders and parents understand well this simple phrase:

Don't use people to build projects, use projects to build people.

Taking time to work together on projects is not always

efficient. Teaching skills and giving out real responsibility early, or delegating tasks to others that you can do better and faster, can result in embarrassment and messes that you have to clean up. The upshot can be a confident and experienced next-generation ready to push the envelope, battle against cultural decay and take on "giants" that you never would have been able to face.

* * * * * * * * * * *

questions for reflection:

- *What are your top two values when it comes to finances? How are you passing those on to your next generation?*

- *How are you and those who look to you for leadership being challenged just beyond your and their abilities?*

- *How could the concept of pre-teen challenges be applied to training up apprentices, interns or novices in your workplace?*

chapter seven endnotes

[37] Robert Dohrenwend *The Sling: Forgotten Firepower of Antiquity* (2002) p 40.

[38] ibid

[39] Dave and Claudia Arp. *Giant Steps.* (1994).

[40] As quoted by Loren Cunningham in personal conversation (2006).

[41] Michael A. Valles. *Your Complete Guide to Leaving an Inheritance for Your Children and Others.* (2008). p 207.

CHAPTER EIGHT

Making 3G Work for You

No one can be excellent by themselves.

-Coach Carter

We have talked a lot about how 3G has worked in our own family. What about your leadership team, your "disciples?" Can 3G work for you?

You have riches to leave to your inheritors! Even your failures, processed well and communicated to the next generation, can catapult them ahead of their peers.

We can draw encouragement from Thomas Edison. When asked about developing the electric light bulb, he admitted to a few defeats! His conclusion:

> *I have not failed. I've just found 10,000 ways that won't work![42]*

So how do you begin a 3G legacy? A good starting point is to identify your five to seven most important core values. What character traits would you want someone to exhibit who is called by your last name or works for your company?

Now, before you read further, take this task on seriously. Get out a piece of paper, start a note on your electronic device or use the space at the end of this chapter, and think this question through. What is important to you? What do you want your progeny, whether children or followers, to carry with them when you're gone? You can see our family's list in the endnotes of this chapter,[43] but I don't want you to be distracted from what are truly *your* core values. Honesty? Generosity? Resilience? Humility? Take a moment to reflect and put them in the best order you can.

Try to distill your thoughts into values, not just positive actions you wish you were doing or negative actions to avoid. For instance, you might choose, "Have a perfect heart and always forgive." Sounds great, but unless you are Jesus, this may not describe your life and character. It's an aspiration but not a value of your life to pass on. Or you may put down, "Don't call people bad names." That's an action to avoid but what is the root value? "Be free from prejudice," "Respect people regardless" or "Love your neighbor as yourself" might be better value statements. Try to break your thoughts down to positive root virtues/values.

Now try it. It will perhaps require a few minutes of reflection. Don't worry about being perfect, you can change and refine your list later.

Got it? Let this serve as a base as we work through some exercises to build and execute a 3G strategy. (Yes, of course, you can read on without writing your core values down ... this is your book! But it will be helpful if you have something concrete as we work through this chapter.)

How will this list help you? First, it can serve as a guideline for when to intervene and when to let something slide. Someone gave us good advice years ago when our children were teenagers. They said it's vitally important to "choose your battles" when raising adolescents. This applies to leading anyone! Maybe their hair is too long (think the '70s) or their music too loud, or they have a fixation with the color black. And what if they still haven't learned to clean up their room, or they seem unable to deliver any work on time? Which of these is a stop-everything-sit-down-this-is-serious situation, and which is problematic but perhaps something they will outgrow?

> It's vitally important to "choose your battles" when raising adolescents. This applies to leading anyone!

3G Helps Solve a Fashion Question

In the early millennial years, it was quite fashionable for guys and gals to sport the "gangsta" look, wearing their pants low so everyone could see their brand of underwear and a lot more! This was great for Calvin Klein but distressing to many moms and dads. Why? That's the important question a 3G parent asks before acting. Why am I so angry? What causes me to want to whack them up the side of the head?

Is it because I feel embarrassed as their parent? Then the real reason I'm lashing out is because the value in play is my comfort and reputation. More thought is needed before you bring down hellfire and brimstone on them. Perhaps another will say, "They need to be modest!" True, but why? Because there are plenty of evil people out there with prying eyes? Also true, but is there a deeper value involved? What if your root value is that we are created in God's image and we should honor everyone, including ourselves? This might give you a little more traction as you approach this delicate "fashion" issue. It might change this conversation: "Connie, you're not leaving this house dressed like a tramp! Get back in there and change into something decent!" into something like this: "Connie, that seems to be a new fashion for you, to show off your underwear brand. Can you tell me a little about it?"

"Oh, Mom!" will be a typical response.

"I'm just wondering, when attention gets so focused on your posterior, how might that help people know and respect the real Connie you are inside?"

Your involvement is not based on personal embarrassment or anger, but on relating values to the issue at hand. The discussion might very well end there with another exasperated groan of frustration, or it may just open up a teachable moment. Either way, the questions and interventions are linked to your core values. And if those values have been discussed, illustrated and lived out in other contexts, that conversation will not soon be forgotten and may lead into deeper considerations that will protect that daughter when the parents aren't around.

Loving Your Teacher as Yourself

Let's take another fairly universal value that may already be on your list and run it through a variety of real situations.

Suppose one of your core values is the biblical axiom, "Love your neighbor as yourself." You believe in it. You try to practice it fairly well with everyone. You desperately hope it will somehow be "caught" by those around you.

Your ten-year-old daughter comes home from school with a dark look shadowing her normally bright young face. At first, she says nothing, but then, through a flood of tears, she declares that her teacher is incredibly unfair because she has accused her of cheating when she didn't do anything wrong.

If you're a parent, you can already feel the steam rising! A typical 2G reaction might be, "Give me the phone number of the professor! I've got a thing or two I would like to tell her!" A 1G parent would simply ignore it. "It's okay! That just happens sometimes." A 3Ger's first reflex is to hear as much of the story as possible before drawing conclusions. "Tell me what happened."

Once you catch the background—your daughter asked her classmate if it would be okay to request permission to go to the bathroom while taking an exam, and the teacher supposed that they were cheating—you begin to flip through your value set and ask yourself, "What principle applies to this situation?" If "love your neighbor as yourself" loosely translated as "put yourself in the other person's shoes" rings the bell, you might venture a question like this, "What do you think might have caused your teacher to react that way?"

"I don't know. All day long, she was just, like, angry with everybody. It's not fair!"

To which you might reply, "Okay, she got angry and took it out on you and it wasn't fair."

Now, here is the link of the situation to underlying values: "When you're angry, do you ever say unkind things to your friends? How do you want your friends to react to you when you say unfair things?"

If your central set of values have a Christian base you might continue: "Have you ever thought about praying for your teachers?"

I remember a conversation almost exactly like this with our third child, Kindra, at about that age. It really does work!

You could change the situation to an employee complaining about a co-worker, a parishioner who doesn't like the pastor's preaching, or a wife frustrated by a critical husband. Firing the employee, dismissing the preacher or beating up the offending

husband may temporarily *fix* the problem but it will not *affix*
the value in the heart of the
person. They will not have
gained any tools to win the next
battle. These employees and
offspring will either become
more dependent upon you to
keep solving their problems or
simply run away from similar
conflict in the future. To say it
once more: a 2G response attempts to *fix* the situation; a 3G
response attempts to use the situation to *affix* a value.

> A 2G response attempts to *fix* the situation; a 3G response attempts to use the situation to *affix* a value.

At first, you may need a moment to do this mental exercise
of sifting through your values and asking yourself which ones
are most pertinent to the particular situation. Sometimes it
helps to literally count to ten or ask the offending party to give
you a moment to think before responding. With practice, the
process can become natural and automatic. In some
situations, you may find that *no particular value* is being
violated or illustrated. Remember the story of Dale Kauffman's
young son spilling breakfast on him in chapter five? Extremely
bad timing caused real physical damage to a new suit and
messed up a carefully planned adult schedule. However, it was
purely an accident that did not require sanctions or a long
lecture, just a big hug.

The more you know your values, the easier it is to
discipline. Robert Schuller once said, "It's not difficult to make
decisions when you have no conflicts in your value system."[44]
Surely easier said than done!

Developing a Generous Heart

Let's suppose another of your core values is generosity.

This is a tough one, especially for younger children. I think of the mother who prepared a delicious pancake breakfast for her seven-year-old and five-year-old sons. When they began to argue over who would get the first pancake, the wise mom saw an opportunity for a moral lesson. "If Jesus were sitting here, He would say, 'Let my brother have the first pancake, I can wait.'" The older brother nodded thoughtfully, then turned to his younger sibling and said, "Okay, you be Jesus and let me have the first pancake!"

How do you instill generosity in a second generation? I remember talking with one young lady whose missionary parents always invited people of all kinds into their home. Instead of developing a similar virtue, their children deeply resented the almost daily intrusion into their family life. Instead of a love for hospitality, they inherited a lust for privacy. Good value-passing begins with setting a good example but doesn't end there.

Some friends of ours from Switzerland were pondering this issue of how to reinforce generosity in their second generation. They decided to take a family vacation trip to Romania—with a bread truck! They were given use of a portable bakery on wheels, which they took to an impoverished area of post-communist Romania. All day long for a week they baked and gave away bread loaves to people lined up for hours. It was exhausting but exhilarating. There's always something special about giving and not expecting anything in return. They lived a family experience in raw generosity.

Together they saw grateful smiles of hungry poor humbly receiving their gift. They watched others abuse the privilege by cutting into the line multiple times and observed still others simply take the free bread and leave. For a sweltering week they lived the scriptural admonition, "It's better to give than to receive," and, pardon the pun, they "baked in" values that will never be forgotten.

Want to teach generosity? Romania may be out of reach for you, but what about the local soup kitchen, the yearly Thanksgiving dinner for the homeless, the blood drive, or pushing wheelchairs of the disabled to an event? It may cost time, planning and money, but isn't an investment in your future generations worth it?

Here's one idea you can do right now:

A friend of ours runs an initiative called *LifeRice*. They have developed a program where organizations (schools, businesses, churches, etc.) can sign up to package hyper-nutritious cereal and rice into individual meal packets. Each group buys the rice with vitamin-rich supplements and chooses a day and time to pack and load the food into containers. *LifeRice* then ships it to some of the neediest places on the planet. It's a great way to involve old and young, bosses and employees together in a meaningful project that benefits all. They operate almost anywhere in the US and are now expanding overseas. A great way to do some 3G solidarity! Check it out at: www.liferice.org.

This is 3G and it is within your grasp!

The Power of Affirmation

I don't think we can ever overemphasize the role of affirmation in helping others form good values and character.

There is an old story of two kids named Johnny who were both in the same grade but different classrooms. One Johnny was a terror, a cause for early retirement for more than one teacher. The other was an angel, a model student pulling down straight-A's in every subject. On teacher conference day, the parents of the two Johnnys somehow went to the wrong classrooms—the mother of Johnny the Terror went to the teacher of Johnny the Angel and vice versa.

When both parents returned home, their respective Johnny asked them what their teacher had said. Terrible Johnny was shocked when Mom told him that his teacher lavished praise on him, calling him the best student in his class. He was speechless! "Did she really say that about me?" he wondered. "Yes, and there's more," his mom continued.

Meanwhile, Angelic Johnny was also surprised when his mother told him of the bad report received from his teacher. "This can't be true!" he murmured to himself. The result? Johnny the Terror immediately began to act differently. If his teacher thought he was doing well, there was much more he could show her.[45] His grades began to improve, his motivation increased. The other Johnny had a reasonably good support system already, went back and straightened things out with his teacher, and continued to do well.

Moral of the story? In order to thrive, we all need encouraging people to call us out of our insecurities and self-doubt.

The Magic Ratio

A number of studies have arrived at almost identical conclusions regarding our needs for affirmation. According to psychologist John Gottman's famous experiment with newlyweds, both wives and husbands need a "magic ratio" of at least five positive comments for every negative one:

> *In a fascinating study, Dr. John Gottman teamed up with two mathematicians to test this model. Starting in 1992, they recruited 700 couples who had just received their marriage licenses. For each couple, the researchers videotaped a 15-*

minute conversation between husband and wife and counted the number of positive and negative interactions. Then, based on the 5 to 1 ratio (the "magic ratio" of positive to negative comments needed to produce a healthy marriage relationship), they predicted whether each couple would stay together or divorce.

Ten years later, Gottman and his colleagues followed up with each couple to determine the accuracy of their original predictions. The results were stunning. They had predicted divorce with 94% accuracy—based on scoring the couples' interactions for 15 minutes.[46]

A more recent study tracking brain reactions confirms this human emotional need. According to Nobel Laureate Daniel Kahneman:

Each day we experience approximately 20,000 moments. A moment is defined as a few seconds in which our brain records an experience. The quality of our days is determined by how our brains recognize and categorize our moments— either as positive, negative, or just neutral. Rarely do we remember neutral moments. Now scientists propose that each day our brains—i.e., our thoughts and emotions—keep track of our positive and negative moments, and the resulting score contributes to our overall mood.[47]

Studies in the workplace[48] about praise-to-criticism ratios come to similar conclusions, identifying nearly the same "magic ratio" as Gottman's.

Filling Our Buckets

Donald O. Clifton and Tom Rath, a grandfather/grandson team, use the metaphor of a bucket and dipper in their book, *How Full Is Your Bucket?* to emphasize this idea:

> *Imagine we all have a bucket within us that needs to be filled with positive experiences, such as recognition or praise. When we're negative toward others, we use a dipper to remove from their buckets and diminish their positive outlook. When we treat others in a positive manner, we fill not only their buckets but ours as well.*[49]

Everyone needs an encourager, a "releaser," someone to call them out publicly and say, "You're the man! This is your moment! Carpe diem!" A friend of mine used to say, "It took John the Baptist to get Jesus out of the carpenter shop." When John the Baptist famously called out to Jesus at the river Jordan, "Behold, the Lamb of God who takes away the sin of the world!"[50] Jesus could never go back to his day job. He was marked and lifted up by his cousin to seize the day and live out his destiny. In Queen Esther's enduring story, the basis for the Jewish feast of Purim, her cousin Mordecai declares to the young queen that she was born for "such a time as this," lending courage to risk her life and approach the king to intercede for the salvation of her people.

The celebrated pianist Lang Lang revealed in a recent interview[51] that when he was nine years old, his piano teacher told him he would never amount to anything and should quit taking lessons. Millions around the world, touched by his exuberant music, are glad another voice encouraged him on.

Can you think of someone in your journey who encouraged you and called you out? Was there a time in your life when a mentor or friend took you aside and said, "I believe in you!"?

For some, the first great "release" was when we heard the gentle words of the Scriptures telling us that even while we were yet sinners, our Creator loved us and considered us of such value He was willing to sacrifice all to get us back.[52] Prostitutes, prodigal sons and daughters, murderers and cheaters, business leaders and beggars all needed to hear those words, "You have value! I believe in you!" Likewise, a 3G leader or parent is always on the lookout for key moments to encourage, support and affirm.

Bill Johnson, a world-renowned Christian leader, shares this anecdote from his family:

> *Children learn what's important to us by seeing what we get excited about in their lives—both negatively and positively. I remember watching one of my sons treating his brother with unusual kindness. I stopped him and said, "Son, do you know what that was?" He looked at me like he was in trouble. "That was kindness!" I continued, "That is a fruit of the Spirit. Great job on how you treated your brother."[53]*

If your child, employee or follower has "an empty bucket," and receives more negative than positive comments from you, how can they embrace your values when you're also their source of so much negative feedback? It just doesn't work.

Why not start talking 3G now? Consider someone you influence, someone of your second generation, who could use a little more "water in their bucket." Go and tell them one or two affirmations, true, precise and vocal praise based on something you have observed them do or say. "You did a great job taking out that garbage—no spills!" "I like the way you come in with a smile every morning!" "The kind words you said to me yesterday were appreciated deeply. You made my day!"

The well is bottomless, but it takes intentional effort to insert your "dipper" and pour out to another.

* * * * * * * * * *

questions for reflection

- *What are your five to seven most important key values?*

1.

2.

3.

4.

5.

6.

7.

- *Who was someone who acted as "releaser" in your journey? How did they do it? Who needs you to call them out and release them?*

- *Who, in your circle of influence, could use some "water in their bucket?" Think about one or two affirmations—true, precise and vocal praise based on something you have observed from them, and decide when and how you could fill 'em up!*

chapter eight endnotes

---

[42] Elkhorne, J.L. *Edison—The Fabulous Drone, in 73* Vol. XLVI, No. 3 (March 1967), p. 52

[43] Clewett Family Values:
1. Get in and stay in right relationship with God
2. Generous lifestyle
3. Integrity in what you say and do
4. Develop a sense of humor
5. Go for excellence, never just "good enough"
6. Lead by serving
7. Tithing is the start of financial prudence

[44] Heard live in a message in Orange, CA 1989

[45] This phenomenon is called the "Pygmalion effect" in education or "self-fulfilling prophecy" in psychological circles.

[46] http://www.gallup.com/businessjournal/12916/big-impact-small-interactions.aspx

[47] http://www.ocde.us/PBIS/Documents/Articles/Positive+$!26+Negative+Ratio.pdf

[48] Jack Zenger and Joseph Folkman. *Ideal Praise to Criticism Ratio - (2013)*

[49] Donald O. Clifton and Tom Rath. *How Full is Your Bucket?" (2004)*

[50] *John 1:29*

[51] http://www.lavanguardia.com/cultura/20160707/403015624216/hay-que-tener-fe-porque-cada-dia-es-un-nuevo-concierto.html

[52] *Romans 5:8, But God demonstrates His own love toward us, in that while we were yet sinners, Christ died for us.*

[53] Danny Silk, *Loving Our Kids on Purpose.* (2013). p6

CHAPTER NINE

Bucking Generational Trends

He gave us wings to soar.

-*Rich Clewett*

As stated earlier, each generation shares certain generalized characteristics. Sometimes they are good ones, like the "heroic" virtues that sociologists observe in the generation who lived through World War II. The survivors built cities, raised families and formed economies based on hard-earned values and a clear understanding of good and evil.

Their children, however, my own "baby boomer" generation, generally held a radically different worldview. We were used to privilege and security with no enemy threat or war shadowing our coastlines. We ripped apart almost every value and institution for which our parents had fought—family, religion, government, progress—like a child tearing into a Snickers bar, and asked, "Why?"

John Lennon's song "Imagine" deconstructed almost every important belief of the previous generation. "Imagine there's no countries, nothing to kill or die for, no religion, too." In one ingenuous tune, the Beatles songwriter distanced children from their heroic parents, told them the war they had won was useless, and that any sense of good versus evil was not worth dying for. That was incomprehensible to those who freed starving prisoners from Jewish concentration camps and witnessed the savagery of Japanese lust for world domination. A "generation gap" widened. Baby boomers veered into drugs and free love while their parents wondered what happened.

William Strauss and Neil Howe, in their landmark study *Generations*[54] have uncovered predictable and repeating patterns from generation to generation. Their exhaustive review of five hundred years of American history reveals a four-generation sequence they call a *generational constellation*. In other words, after every four generations, or about eighty-four years, the basic characteristics found in the first generation were repeated in the fifth, and the cycle started over again. Their research is substantial and remarkable. They demonstrate convincingly that the children of a Civic generation (their label for my World War II veteran dad's generation) will tend to be *Idealist*, believing that the world's great problems can probably be solved by music, art, and other peaceful expressions. Imagine that!

Interestingly, this four-generation cycle is not just limited to America but has also been identified by historians in other countries, notably the 19th century writers Émile Littré and Giuseppe Ferrari, and more recently by Spanish sociologist Julián Marías and American historian Samuel Huntington.[55]

Here's something to watch for: Following their four-generation cycle theory, Strauss and Howe went out on a limb to predict that the next major social crisis along the lines of a world war or national disaster will probably occur within a few years of 2020, and that the next Great Generation will be the Millenials now in their twenties and thirties[56] We'll see how that prediction plays out in the coming years!

Wow !

Strauss and Howe's research and conclusions are truly fascinating for students of history but well beyond the scope of analysis in these pages.

I cite this material to simply recognize the tectonic forces pushing and pulling our students, children and followers into patterns that can be either destructive or useful. <u>Giving them tools to discern and resist negative peer pressure is vital</u> for all leaders, regardless of their generational identity.

3G thinking is imperative to help the next generation keep a steady course through ever-shifting social and moral seas. Concerned 2G leaders will tend to protect and even isolate their offspring and followers from what they see as harmful influences. "No, you can't dress like that! No, you can't listen to that style of music! Why do you want to wear all black and do your hair like Amy Winehouse?" They know what good music, proper clothing and hairstyles should be from their generational experience. The best way to make sure their next generation grows up wholesome, they believe, is to eliminate all bad influences and restrict access to media that promotes such things. But it doesn't work very often.

Trying to protect against the deep currents of generational trends is like filling up sandbags when you see a tsunami on the horizon. By then, it's too late. Their beliefs and values need to be built before the waves crash and then be affirmed as the sea rises.

2G spiritual leaders often label any new technology as a "tool of the Devil." Because of these newfangled personal electronic devices, their followers are listening to and watching things they shouldn't! It is true statement that historically, pornographers are always the first to exploit new media, from the dawn of radio to streaming downloads. But blaming the media technology itself is directing fire at the wrong target. It's like shooting the messenger who brings bad news. Technology is merely the messenger, not the enemy. Here's what some tech authorities say about new technologies and their moral value:

> *We offer two basic morals. The first is that technology is inherently neither good or bad—it can be used for good or ill, to free us or to shackle us. Second, new technology brings social change, and change comes with both risks and opportunities.*[57]

Parents in the '60s couldn't understand why otherwise intelligent young people attached the new transistor radio to their ears and listened to music all day long instead of studying to be an engineer. School teachers in the late '60s and '70s were horrified by a massive teenage slide into drugs and "open" moral standards. As I write this in 2017, almost anyone over forty years old just doesn't understand the lure of social networks and the addict-like urge to check into the newest Facebook, Instagram, Snapchat or whatever emerging platform carries the posts of their friends. To us, it's a colossal waste of time. To them it is an umbilical cord of life.

In my growing up years, rock music and long hair were the enemy of every caring school teacher, spiritual leader and parent. The Beatles and the Stones were outlawed from our house and church. Discussions raged about exactly what length of hair distinguished normal people from hippies.

I'm thankful that my parents somehow looked beyond my afro hairstyle (I have pictures!), Beatles albums (my brother secretly purchased a few!) and tie-dyed shirts. They kept up a constant stream of encouragement, supporting me in almost every adolescent pursuit. I'm sure they skipped a heartbeat or two when we hummed covert tunes about drugs ("Lucy in the

Sky with Diamonds" the Beatle's famous hit, was a barely disguised praise to LSD), wore our hair in strange ways and attended high school dances where the odor of cannabis hung heavy in the air. Yet I can't remember a discouraging word from those years. They didn't equate outward expressions with bad values. I'm thankful for that, because in the early 70s, the lines began to blur.

On the West Coast of California, hippies began flushing drugs down the toilet, carrying Bibles, and pointing index fingers instead of their middle fingers upward, indicating "One Way!" as the Jesus Movement caught fire. Parents and leaders were not quite sure where to point their children and followers during those turbulent years of protest and praise. Christian "communes" sprang up where latent marijuana smoke and rock worship music rose skyward together. Electric guitars and drums entered church sanctuaries, scandalizing many spiritual leaders and delighting as many others. How could parents and moral guardians "protect and direct" their charges in this dizzying mix?

That's just the point—they couldn't!

At our father's funeral in 2007, my oldest brother described that parental process with a phrase that has become part of my own 3G vocabulary. He probably doesn't even remember, but in front of over five hundred gathered friends and family in Kona, Hawaii, amid casket and flowers, he said, "My dad gave us wings to soar."

Wings to soar—I like that! Are we controlling the following generation with chains or giving them wings to soar? Chains or wings? This simple analogy describes the contrast between 2G and 3G thinking. We can send out children and followers who are "driven and tossed"[58] by every new trend offered by their generational gurus, or we can give them a clear moral compass to navigate the storms ahead.

"Trending" is trendy right now as I am writing these pages. You can go to a social networking site like Facebook and find out immediately what is "trending" around the world. With one keystroke you can discover what millions of people are searching for at any given moment.

It's the ultimate annihilation of creativity and resolve. Instead of contemplating what is real and right, a person can be swept up in whatever is the current trend. It may last only seconds but confirms you as part of the collective generational mindset.

So how do we help our offspring and our future leaders decide which fads are useful and which ones are a detour from their destiny? How can we give them tools to resist the almighty "peer pressure" threatening to deform their conscience and heritage? How can we help them buck generational trends?

In the next chapter, we will examine three tools you can use to help your next generations establish their identity and build healthy values: Questions, Stories, and Food.

✳ ✳ ✳ ✳ ✳ ✳ ✳ ✳ ✳ ✳ ✳

questions for reflection

- *What words would you use to describe your generation in light of the studies by Strauss and Howe?*

- *If you had the ability to "wish away" one generational trend, which one would you choose to eject into outer space, never to be bothered with again?*

- *What is the value that you would replace it with? How can you model and help affix that value onto others?*

chapter nine endnotes

[54] William Strauss & Neil Howe. *Generations.* (1991)

[55] ibid p 104

[56] See Strauss and Howe's following Volume, *Millenials Rising*

[57] Hal Abelson, Ken Ledeen and Harry Lewis. *Blown to Bits: Your Life, Liberty and Happiness After the Digital Explosion,* (2008) p14

[58] From *James 1:6 ...for the one who doubts is like the surf of the sea, driven and tossed by the wind.*

CHAPTER TEN

Tools for Your Toolkit: Questions, Stories, Food

"Go home and love your family!"
-Mother Theresa, accepting the Nobel Prize,
answers about how to promote world peace.

The Power of Questions

My wife, Patti, is a professional life-coach. Every week she coaches leaders and trains others to do the same around the world. Both her and my leadership styles have been profoundly altered by applying simple coaching principles to the way we lead, especially in how we ask questions. We have discovered that questions answered with a yes or a no are called *closed questions*. Closed questions literally stop the thinking process. They force the responder to follow the questioner's agenda, defrauding both of the chance to tap the heart issues.

Let's suppose your eighteen-year-old comes home two hours late and you assume he has been at that party you expressly forbade him to attend. You could start your tirade with, "Don't you realize what a stupid thing you just did?" Closed question! He can answer yes or no, but either one will only heap coals on your already smoldering fire. You could continue with, "Didn't you stop to think about your final exams tomorrow?"

We pretty much know how this conversation will go—producing an irate parent and an even more withdrawn teen. What may not be so clear are the likely long-term effects of such interrogation techniques: a) He will be even more sneaky next time he wants to venture outside parental limits or, b) He will back down a few notches on his creativity and independence, fearing another outburst, and become just a little more dependent on you to make his decisions and set his standards.

Open questions, on the other hand, allow the responder to fill in the details. They open the door to explore what really happened and how they felt about it. Let's take the same situation and try an "open question" approach:

"John, can you tell me where you have been the last two hours?"

Likely response: "Uh, yeah, Mom, I, uh, just lost track of time while studying at Tim's place."

So far so good. He may be lying or telling the truth, but he's doing the talking, not you. However, here is where we usually slip back into closed questions. "What? Don't you remember me specifically telling you to be home by eleven?" (Closed!) "Were you really at Timmy's house?" (Closed and dangerous to answer!) What if you continued instead with a question like this:

"John, we were really expecting you to return by eleven. When you arrive two hours late without any communication, how do you think that makes us feel?"

Do you see the subtle shift away from blame and punishment to considering his and your welfare? Values of safety, honor, protection, love, and family care could easily break into the dialogue. You might even be able to broach the subject of disobedience this way:

"John, you know that your father and I were quite concerned about you possibly going to that party at Marty's house." Here are two choices for finishing this question. You decide which one will get a better answer: "Did you?" or "Can you tell me how you felt about that restriction and if it had any bearing on your late arrival?"

Open questions can determine whether the encounter results in a teachable moment or another sullen teenager and further distance between parents and their offspring.

Here's what William P. Young, best selling author of *The Shack*,[59] says about questions for your second generation:

> *A question is an invitation into relationship and one good question is worth a thousand answers. Their response will be a window into the uniqueness of your child, how they think and what their emotional world looks like. "How do you think that works? Why do you think they said that? Who do you think we could ask who might know? How did that make you feel?" Questions open up the world; for you, your child and your growing relationship.*[60]

We could easily insert "student," "follower," or "co-worker" for "child" in Young's comments above. When we mine another's thoughts and feelings instead of imposing our own, we help our next generation make decisions based on their own set of emerging values.

When we have a preconceived idea of the motivation behind someone's behavior, when intimidation and closed questions are our tools of inquiry, we don't always discover the truth. Often the problem is quite different from our assumptions.

What if John had been out doing some late shopping for *your* birthday gift? What if there had been an accident and John heroically saved a classmate's life, or he really was studying at Tim's house? Assuming there is at least good motivation, if not good reason, behind another's fault is a life skill worth learning.

Master motivator Tony Robbins says:

> *It's not the events of your life that determine how you feel and act but, rather, the meaning you create from your life's experiences. Learning to ask empowering questions—especially in moments of crisis—is a critical skill that will ultimately shape the meanings you create, and therefore the quality of your life.*[61]

Let open questions be a valued part of your 3G toolkit. Good open questions generally begin with who, what, where, when, why, or how. Here are great examples of open questions drawn from professional coaches around the world:[62]

- *What's holding you back?*
  —Jenny Leow

- *What are you trying to prove to yourself?*
  —Jessica Malavez

- *How does this decision match up with who you know you are?*
  —Rebecca Macfarlane

- *If I was in your shoes and asked for advice, what would be the first thing you'd tell me?*
  —Thom J. Ferrie

- *What would you try now if you knew you could not fail?*
  —Alyssa Gonzalez

- *When will you start?*
  —Pat Kennedy

- *What small steps can you take to get you closer to your vision?*
  —Josephine de la Paz

- *What do you think the moral of that story is?*
  —Brent Nestler

- *What am I not asking you that you really want me to ask?*
  —Annie Gelfand

These are great questions posed by seasoned pros. You can memorize a few of these or begin by retraining your conversation habits. In tense moments, pause and retool that closed question—"Are you going to change that bad attitude?"—into an open one just by changing the interrogative word: "How can you begin an attitude change?" "What's preventing you from taking these steps we just talked about?" "When would you like to take the first step?"

Good questions lead to values-based discussions and actions. Bad questions lead to more conflict.

The Impact of Stories

Einstein's off-the-cuff remarks about stories bears repeating:

> *If you want your children to be smart, tell them fiary tales. If you want them to be really smart, tell them more fairy tales. If you want your children to be brilliant, tell them even more fairy tales.*[63]

A picture may be worth a thousand words, but a well-told story, a "word-picture," may be worth even more. When someone views a photograph or a realistic painting, they see what the photographer or artist saw when they tripped the shutter or ran a brush over canvas. When someone tells a story, the image in the storyteller's mind is linked to the imagination of the listener's mind. Impressions received are often quite different from the storyteller's image. Like a Monet or Renoir impressionist painting, stories are designed to evoke a feeling and/or provoke reaction rather than simply copy a given reality.

A good story links imagery with emotion and is one of the more important ways to instill family values or organizational goals into your team. It can be real or made up, as long as you let them know which is fiction!

Here's a question for parents. Do your children know your love story: how you met your spouse, the funny and even stupid things you did? If you are people of faith, do they know your conversion testimony—what key events happened to you that led you to an unshakable commitment? These are two bedrocks of your family and their identity. Yet we find that many parents never tell these stories.

Every organization has anecdotes of how they got started. How they began with a pencil drawing on a napkin, the first big goofs, the lucky break that got them going. Business leaders know the importance of retelling these tales. In German, these are called the *Heilige Geschichte* or "Holy Story" of the beginning of any enterprise. Telling and retelling these histories draws others into the inner circle. Hearing about the early beginnings helps new arrivals understand the reasons why we do things the way we do and forges bonds of identity and common ground with old hands.

Stories can be funny ("Did I ever tell you about the dance lessons your mom and I took?") or serious ("Do you know what happened last week when a guy about your age refused to put on his seatbelt?"). They can be long stem-winders or short anecdotes. Good tales include names, dates, colors, smells, tastes and noises. Better stories include interesting characters, dramatic tension, conflict and problem solving. They attach themselves to the imagination of the hearers, open up worlds and seal values in place.

When our kids were growing up, we often carried CDs of *Adventures in Odyssey,* a fictional values-heavy audio series produced by Focus on the Family, on our innumerable long trips across Spain and around the world. The kids would put on their earphones and listen contentedly for hours. This was a wonderful break for us and apparently some teachable moments for them.

I remember once being seated at the dinner table in our Barcelona apartment talking about some concern of our older children when our five-year-old Cristina piped up, "That's just adolescent trauma!" *Adolescent trauma?* Those are not words normally tumbling from a kindergartener's mouth. "Where did you hear that?" we asked incredulously. "Odyssey!" she one-worded us back. Later, critical issues about cheating at school or defending the weak also found helpful answers in something they had heard on Odyssey. These dramatized stories fired up their imaginations and quickset memories in their still-soft foundational values.

The Bible tells us what happened to the generation that came after the amazing Israelites who crossed the Jordan and conquered the Promised Land:

> *All that generation also were gathered to their fathers; and there arose another generation after them who did not know the LORD, nor yet the work which He had done for Israel. (Judges 2:10)*

Somewhere in the business of settling a new land and building a nation, Abraham's posterity stopped telling stories. Within a generation they forgot where they came from and Who had led them out of Egypt. The narrative continues:

> *They forsook the LORD, the God of their fathers, who had brought them out of the land of Egypt, and followed other gods from among the gods of the peoples who were around them, and bowed themselves down to them; thus they provoked the LORD to anger. (Judges 2:12)*

Reading books at bedtime, acting out sketches, visiting your family heritage sites and telling the backstory—these activities stamp memories much deeper than any seminar. Use the power of stories in building a 3G heritage!

Let's Eat!

Families at mealtime: the great missing chapter of the 21st century.

Cultural shifts in the last quarter century have cut deeply into the staple 3G habit of earlier generations: eating food together. It's not easy to coordinate schedules when both parents work, often at different shifts. Always-on electronic devices and the need to check our social networks lure us away from the family table. Flexible school scheduling, night classes, after-school sports and pickier eating habits have all cut into these vital values-passing moments of earlier generations.

> Cultural shifts have cut deeply into the staple 3G habit of earlier generations: eating food together.

A recent study in the UK revealed that 10 percent of families never have a meal together during the week and less than a third of Brits sit down every night to dine together.[64] According to the Food Marketing Institute in the US, just 40 percent of American families eat dinner together, and then, no more than two or three times a week. That's in stark contrast to just a generation ago when close to 80 percent of families regularly ate evening meals together.[65]

What is so important about eating meals together? The US National Center on Addiction and Substance Abuse found that kids and teens who share family dinners three or more times per week:

- Are less likely to be overweight
- Are more likely to eat healthy food
- Perform better academically
- Are less likely to engage in risky behaviors (drugs, alcohol, sexual activity)
- Have better relationships with their parents [66]

Why is eating together as good or better than even diet and exercise, according to this study? Brad Watson offers this Theology of Food:

> *Humans have a unique connection with food. We depend on it to survive. We also turn to it for comfort and safety in overindulgence. Food, for some of us, becomes a medium for expressing our creativity, becoming art. Fundamentally, food reminds us of our need for something outside of ourselves. We have to take, receive, and eat to continue moving through this world.*
>
> *At the table, we share our stories, we listen to one another, and we experience grace. The New Testament describes this act as "breaking bread" and invokes a giving and receiving of relationship in the most simple and unspoken of ways. The communal meal begins through arrival or gathering. This is the moment when everyone's individual responsibilities, schedules,*

and to-do lists collide into an expression of community. The worries, struggles, fears, and happy news of each member comes rushing through the door. Your lives are hurried until this point. Your lives are physically separate until this moment ... You are physically united by the table you gather around, the complete meal everyone shares in.[67]

Most people know how to eat. Although some may demand the proper silverware and jut their pinky out when drinking tea, everyone eats. The act of putting food in your mouth is a classless activity. By nature, it is an act of giving and receiving, as Watson points out. With hands busy, minds are freed to survey the events of the day and, intentionally or not, link values and provide opportunity for evaluation. Tim Chester goes so far as to identify eating meals together as a key characteristic of making disciples:

Jesus didn't run projects, establish ministries, create programs, or put on events. He ate meals.[68]

So how do we counter the trend of isolated eating? The easy answer is to cut down on activities that conflict with mealtimes. If that's not possible or practical in your situation, here are some suggestions extracted and updated from Rebecca Sweat's article, *The Family That Eats Together:*[69]

PUT IT ON YOUR CALENDAR: *If family members simply can't rearrange their schedules for regular meals together, create a monthly meal calendar with at least two times a week set* *aside for a family meal. Find times when your family could be together with a minimum of disruptions. "It doesn't have to be an evening dinner," Doherty[70] says. "It could be a Sunday morning breakfast, a late-night dessert, or a snack before bedtime."*

GET EVERYONE INVOLVED: *Get everyone in the family to pitch in with food preparation, table setting and cleanup, so that one person isn't doing all the work. "The whole family can be in the kitchen together, one person setting the table, someone else doing the stir-fry, another making a salad, and everyone can help clean up afterward," suggests Barbara James, an associate professor of family and consumer sciences at Ohio State University. Not only does this spread out the workload, she says; it's also a good opportunity for communication and teaching children how to cook.*

TURN OFF THE ELECTRONICS: *Eat at the dining room table for most meals without a television (or electronic device!) on in the background. Put cell phones on silent and ask friends and family to wait until after the dinner hour or your children's bedtime, unless there's an emergency.*

Be intentional! You could schedule a "family fast-food night" where everyone converges on the same place for a terrible meal but a great family time. Or what about a shared coffee or early breakfast? The time of day doesn't really matter. Being together without other distractions does.

One day soon, our warp-speed Western culture will simply not be able to bear the emotional strain of current lifestyles. I believe we will see a "retro food movement" as people take stock of the damage our current habits cause to the delicate family fabric. One early reader of the manuscript has corrected me by pointing out: "This movement already exists! It's called the 'Slow Movement' or the 'Slow Food Movement,' which aims to address the issue of 'time-poverty' and has over eight hundred chapters worldwide."

Take back the act of corporate meal times. A few years back we had three different organizations operating out of one building. Although all three were involved in similar charitable work, our mostly single and very busy staff members never interrelated. We declared a "family meal time" every Tuesday lunch. One group would be responsible for food preparation and table setting for about thirty of us, and the others would chip in a couple euros to cover the ingredients. Stories were told, friendships emerged and we all began changing our schedules around so we wouldn't miss that shared time each week.

Okay, dear reader. This has been a lot to digest! Are you ready for a break?

Let's take a one-chapter detour to the Northeast corner of Spain. I'd like to introduce you to a unique folkloric tradition of *Catalunya* ("Catalonia" to the English-speaking world) that illustrates 3G in action.

* * * * * * * * * * *

questions for reflection

- *Share your love story with your children or a group of singles from your circle of influence. Include the funny and even stupid things you did.*

- *Use open questions to get mealtime conversations started. Try some of these or make up your own:*

   What was the highlight of your day today?

   What made you laugh today? What did you wonder about? Dream about?

   What made you sad today? How did you deal with that sadness?

chapter ten endnotes

59 *The Shack* is a parable/analogy about love from a divine perspective. It was the No. 1 paperback trade fiction seller on *The New York Times Bestseller List* from June 2008 to early 2010.

60 http://wmpaulyoung.com/parent-by-participation/

61 https://www.tonyrobbins.com/training/power-of-questions/

62 from: https://coachfederation.org/blog/index.php/1806/

63 http://www.azquotes.com/quote/876064

64 Bianca London. Daily Mail Online, Nov 19, 2012. http://www.dailymail.co.uk/femail/article-2235161/Families-manage-sit-dinner-twice-week--10-NEVER-eating-together.html

65 https://www.vision.org/visionmedia/article.aspx%3Fid%3D246

[66] http://www.centeronaddiction.org/addiction-research/reports/importance-of-family-dinners-2012

[67] http://bradawatson.com/2016/05/eating-together/

[68] *http://gcdiscipleship.com/2012/02/06/show-hospitality-share-the-gospel/*

[69] https://www.vision.org/visionmedia/article.aspx%3Fid%3D246

[70] William P. Doherty, Professor and Director of the Marriage and Family Therapy Program at University of Minnesota

The Castellers of Catalunya

We are like dwarfs on shoulders of giants.
-Bernard de Chartres

Imagine human towers ten levels high, where the lowest man bears up to 1500 pounds (700 kilos) of trembling human bodies on his shoulders. Welcome to the *Castellers* of *Catalunya*[71], a tradition dating back more than 200 years and recently named a "Masterpiece of the Oral and Intangible Heritage of Humanity" by UNESCO.[72]

On certain festival days, you will see them in white pants and mono-colored shirts carrying rolled black waist-wraps called *faixas* under their arms; men, women and children running to catch the metro or piling off busses at the public square where they will do their performance. They are all members of different clubs that practice this ancient tradition of climbing on each other's shoulders.

At a leader's signal, a hundred or more human bodies press together, hands raised, forming the *pinya* or foundation of the human structure. The towers they will build have a place for all ages and body types. Stocky men take up the bottom positions, teenagers and twenty-somethings occupy the middle stories, and children as young as five clamber to the top to crown the formation.

When the second story is securely positioned on the shoulders of the base, the crowd of red, green or purple-shirted (depending on their club affiliation) men and women press chest-to-back as tight as they can, arms outstretched to grasp and lock the elbows of the one in front. The ones closest to the developing tower lift their hands like flying buttresses (pun intended!) to push against the buttocks of the second-tier climbers, thus forming a pattern of radial spokes moving out from the base now buried under a sweating mass of humanity. Other women, children, even passers-by, wedge into the spaces between the radials. The foundation must be solid and evenly supported from all directions to bear the vertical pressure to come.

Once middle stories are formed, the leader calls for the last three levels to ascend. The unmistakable reedy sound of the *grallas,* traditional oboe-like instruments, pierce the air as the youngest elements of the formation begin climbing barefoot over the shoulders of the *pinya* to reach the summit.

Helmeted children get one toehold into the corset-tight waist wraps of each wavering body and then lift the other foot onto their shoulders as they ascend each level. The lower stories have from two to five people, but the top two levels are reserved for one person each, generally younger children. The second-to-top climber squats down and finally the topmost element, called the *enxaneta,* straddles his crouched friend and offers a quick salute to the crowds up to forty feet (twenty seven meters) below. Then they slide down the backs of lower layers like firemen down a pole, as quickly as they can before the quaking structure collapses.

top: The Clewett Castellers in 1992.
Bottom: Waist wraps called "faixas" must be snug.

top: *The* pinya *gets set.*
Bottom: The club leader *shouts instructions.*

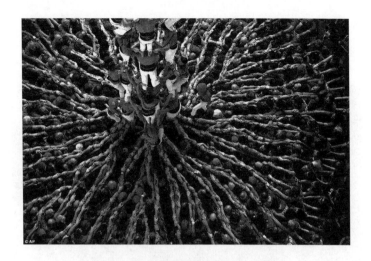

top: View from above!
Bottom: Place for every age.

*The completed castell. Can you count the levels?
(hint: This is a "tres de nou amb folre."*

There is one competition each year where points are scored according to complexity and number of formations each club can build and dismantle without mishap. But castle-building in Catalunya is not so much an athletic competition as a cultural expression and a great object lesson in 3G!

> Castle-building in Catalunya is ... a great object lesson in 3G!

We were introduced to the Castellers in 1991. A friend and I heard the sound of Ping-Pong a few doors down from our apartment in Barcelona. Being a bit bored, we walked into a small bar-cafeteria with posters of human towers plastered on the walls. When we asked about the pictures, they opened a rear door and ushered us into the world of Castellers. We entered a small gym pungent with human sweat. People of all ages milled around, sleeves and pantlegs rolled up, dressed normally except for the black *faixas* around their waists. They jabbered in rapid *Catalán*.[73] A few volunteers interpreted into Spanish for us clueless *norte-americanos*. I asked one of them about the trap door in the ceiling. "Oh, that! You'll see why in just a few minutes," he replied with a twinkle in his eye.

Orders were barked that we didn't understand, and suddenly the unruly crowd became a well-oiled machine with *pinya*, lower layers, and final stories magically emerging from the mass of men, women and children. Sure enough, just before the last youth and children reached their top positions, someone pulled a cable to open the trap door in the ceiling. Why? So that the final climber, the young *enxaneta,* could top off the human tower with his head sticking out above the roof!

Our family became members of the Castellers of Barcelona during the 1992 Olympic year. My son and I took part in the opening ceremonies, an amazing experience. He climbed to the top, clearly visible on TV around the world. I was part of the bottom *pinya*, my personal "moment of glory" when perhaps a billion viewers saw the back of my head for five seconds!

The spectacle of each component standing on the shoulders of the person below, anchored solidly by old veterans, with top position reserved for the youngest generation, is a wonderful life-sized illustration of 3G.

Older adults provide the experience and gravitas to set a firm foundation. Younger adults and teens occupy the middle stories. They're strong but still flexible enough to make slight weight changes to keep the tower growing. Finally, the most visible and vulnerable positions are taken by the youngest members of this extended family. By themselves, they could never rise that high. Built on the shoulders of earlier generations, they can literally go "through the roof!"

Bernard of Chartres first coined the phrase, "We are like dwarfs on the shoulders of giants."[74] This is certainly reason enough to embark on a 3G lifestyle: so your progeny can start where you leave off. Each generation can inherit tools of discernment from the previous one, so those who follow won't have to start at zero. They can jam their toes into your black *faixa*, climb onto your shoulders and be ready to support the following generation. Is it possible to extend through three generations, perhaps even produce a remarkable fourth generation that will change the world? Consider the image of the Castellers!

Each generation can inherit tools of discernment from the previous one so those that follow won't have to start at zero.

One more lesson from this unique cultural expression: No

matter how strong or balanced the initial stage, towers can only go so high without the constant, solid pressure provided by the *pinya*, that extended foundation and support network of other people. The weight of upper levels quickly collapses the formation unless others press in and reinforce the weak points of the most central members.

The old African proverb, "It takes a village to raise a child," points to another aspect of 3G undiscussed until now: the role of other people around you.

There comes a time in the life of every child and the career of every employee when they begin to question and criticize the core values of their authorities. Like a boxer pummeling a heavy bag, they test their emerging strength by probing the convictions of the previous generation. They quickly spot inconsistencies ("Why are you driving at 60mph in this 50mph zone?") and question everything. It is a healthy process. They won't form personal values if they don't understand the reason behind them, but it's definitely exasperating for bosses and parents!

We are not called to build carbon copies of ourselves but rather to contribute our DNA to the next generation's widening pool of experiences.

I remember praying fervently for our children in earlier years that they would find a big brother or big sister figure during their teen years. We could see it coming. We knew there would be a time when our best parental advice and 3G strategies would go unheeded. A storm was already gathering. Just across the horizon lay challenging circumstances that would test their nascent value systems. They were headed for that "dark side of the moon" time of early adolescence when communication blackouts are common. We would need to rely on others who could provide wise counsel and direction.

We are thankful for different older teens and young

professionals who lived in our home, befriended our kids and led their youth groups. These leaders told stories and provided a listening ear in crisis moments that we weren't even aware of until years later!

We all need a *pinya*, no matter how strong we think we are. This can take the form of other parents sharing in a support group, asking for wisdom from grandparents and, yes, even seeking professional counsel or coaching from time to time.

> We all need a *pinya*, no matter how strong we think we are.

To navigate the turbulent waters of adolescence or novice stages in any leadership team, support apart from the parents or primary leader is often required. Does your second generation have that kind of support? Rather than just lamenting how "bad company corrupts good morals," how can we help them find that encouragement and support—that *pinya*?

When our kids finally entered teenage years, we purposely recruited older teens. "Here's five euros. Please take my son out for a coke!" Some would call that bribing, but we were not above that if it meant a positive addition to our child's *pinya*!

Just as novice athletes try to copy everything their sports heroes do, so younger teens hang on every word of older teens and twenty-somethings. In any business, new recruits closely watch old pros for cues. How should I dress? Is the work culture here efficient or laid back? Are questions welcomed or feared by top leadership?

One organization I know head-hunted a top performer who joined the team with one condition. Three others were assigned to acclimatize the new star, by helping him learn the culture, meet other leaders and adapt positively to the new environment.

Find some people that share your values and recruit them! Your posterity may develop a wobble and even collapse if they lack sufficient lateral support. Do whatever is required to ensure your second generation has the *pinya* they need to stay strong and resist peer pressure or the temptation to abandon the heritage you have spent a lifetime developing.

At this point, some may be saying, "Okay, so this is a great illustration. But what happens when the tower has collapsed? What do we do when our second generation takes off on a path of destruction? Is there hope?"

* * * * * * * * * * *

questions for reflection

- *What kind of outside support or "pinya" do your children or followers currently have?*

- *As a single adult, where do you find your regular support system when you face a hard decision or just a lonely time?*

- *Who are you providing support to besides your immediate family? How?*

- *Who are your heroes? Who has been a model for your values and aspirations?*

- *If you can imagine your family as a full body, what part of that body are you?*

chapter eleven endnotes

---

71 Sometimes this region is called *Catalonia* in English but Catalunya is the actual name.

72 http://www.unesco.org/culture/ich/en/RL/human-towers-00364

73 *Catalán,* distinct from Spanish is the native and co-official language of this part of Spain

74 *http://www.goodreads.com/quotes/526239-we-are-like-dwarfs-on-the-shoulders-of-giants-so*

CHAPTER TWELVE

Ruin to Reconciliation: Testimonies of Hope

It is so easy to break down and destroy.
The heroes are those who make peace and
build.

-Nelson Mandela

We talked with quite a few leaders and parents while gathering material for this book. Many encouraged us to get these ideas down on paper and into electronic editions. Others had that faraway look in their eyes that betrayed an aching heart. They agreed that a 3G strategy was great, but these older parents and leaders were in mid-career or the twilight of their lives. Children were grown, followers long since scattered to pursue other concerns. They universally confessed, "I wish we had only known..." and then continued with painful stories of separation and estrangement from their second generation.

Collapsed "towers" and broken relationships were leeching life out of what should be the golden years of appreciation between generations.

The question for them, and perhaps for many others, is not, "What should we have done?" but rather, "What can we do now?"

How can we recover what was lost? Is there hope?

Yes! There is hope!

Will it be quick and easy? No!

What follows is a compilation of testimonies from more than a dozen men and women of different cultures and age groups. Some tell of painful experiences as a child. Others narrate from an adult perspective. All have valuable insights.

Text in *italics* are questions offered by the interviewer to increase clarity. Names have been omitted or changed due to the sensitive nature of each testimony.

In their stories, you will find many of the 3G values already identified in this book. Unconditional love, experiencing life together, family vacations, heaps of affirmation, open questions, developing a *pinya* and intentional evaluation are key stepping stones on the path to reconciliation.

May these real-life stories bring hope to you in your 3G journey, wherever you are!

* * * * * * * * * * *

Disappointed Parents Let their Child "Off the Hook"

Carla, the mom: For years, our son has lived a Bohemian lifestyle, sleeping in his car or hopping from one friend's house to another. We made many attempts to "straighten him out" and help him act responsibly in our way of thinking. But whenever we got together, and it wasn't very often in those days, we would have these explosive, horrible blowups. Some little word would send him off the map saying, "Yeah, that's it! I'm a constant source of disappointment to you guys!" It got to the point where we were like, "Let's just not get together again for a really long time!"

So what helped you to rebuild that relationship?

> As my husband and I began to let ourselves off the hook, we were able to let our son off the hook.

Forgiveness was huge. Forgiving ourselves first and trying to encourage him to forgive himself. As my husband and I began to let ourselves off the hook for the mistakes we made, then we were able to let our son off the hook for the mistakes he made.

I also learned that everybody else's way of raising kids didn't necessarily work for us. Rather than thinking, "How are we gonna shape this life?" we began to ask ourselves how we could support and steward the gifts and abilities that he has.

Sometimes it was confusing. If we affirmed him, did that mean we were agreeing with his lifestyle and decisions? We decided it was okay just to embrace him right where he was. We learned to lift up the things in his life that were good and just not mention the stuff we didn't like. I think that defused things.

We tried not to talk a lot about the past when we were together. We brought back dialogue into the family in little increments. Every time we got together, we became a little more nurturing, more affirming. We virtually went back to how we should have been when he was a little boy. "That's okay. It'll work out. Don't worry about it." It set him free from a lot of self-condemnation!

Darrel, the dad: I realized that constantly communicating the message, "Oh, you're just not making right choices, you're being rebellious," was counter-productive. After all, none of us get it right! I'm still trying to find out what life is all about after more than sixty years!

We just started loving him unconditionally. We didn't expect anything in return, even if it cost us more money.

Mom: We said to each other, "Let's stop being surprised every time these episodes in his life result in financial stress on us. Let's just stop it! Let's figure we will be spending money on him until he is eighty years old. We need to plan an extra reserve to bail him out of his messes." I can't tell you how freeing that was for us!

We have paid his phone bill probably six times in the last two years, but now it's done in a more relational way. He no longer pours guilt on himself over it because now we don't pour it on from our side. He tries much harder to pay us back and we never ever mention the money.

Sometimes we just laid in bed, my husband and I, pained over the latest situation. We had to remind ourselves that no human being would ever love our child more than we, his parents. No one! And here we were, the instruments of his pain, because we were withholding portions of that love. He had enough guilt and shame about his inadequacies that he could pile it on to the point of wanting to kill himself. We didn't need to add into that. We needed to be the ones who say, "No one will ever love you more than we do." Then he could say, "Okay, my guilt and shame are what I am putting on myself. My parents aren't putting it on me. I am." This has helped him over these last ten years to figure out ways to slowly let himself off the hook and make definite steps forward in his life.

Leaving a Leadership Team in Peace or in Pieces

Fred: I was hired by a corporate IT company in Spain to teach English and help bring to market certain software. Soon,

I was named director of sales for the national territory with a team of three sales people and a couple of tech guys. I was making good money and going around to all the finest hotels in Spain doing presentations for corporate customers who thought my American accent meant I was some specialist from the States. I actually didn't even know how the program worked, but that's sales!

Some complaints and backbiting began to arise in our staff. I thought good training and encouraging talk would snuff it out, but I was wrong. Soon, a full-blown break with all kinds of jealousy and distrust poisoned the work atmosphere. Even worse, the others blamed it all on me and my *norte americano* attitude and training ideas. However, I was their boss and figured I would get it worked out somehow.

One day, the corporate vice-president came into town to talk to me and the branch manager. "We are restructuring the office here and it will eliminate two positions. Yours"— pointing to me—"and yours"—pointing to the branch manager. What? We weren't the bad guys! I knew where the trouble was! But the decision was made and we were out!

All kinds of things go through your mind in times like this. Defending yourself, accusing the others, writing mean letters or going up the ladder to speak to the guy above the vice-president.

But another voice was softly saying, "Be still. You can't control or change this. You can only decide how you want to come out on the other end—in peace or in pieces!"

We asked the vice-president to kindly leave the room for a moment and I was shocked when the branch manager turned to me and said, "Isn't this great?"

Great? We had just been unjustly fired!

He went on. "You have some plans to do other things and I do, too. This is our opportunity!"

He was right, but we still needed to act the part. So we put on long faces, asked the VP to come back in and explained to him how poorly this was done. We even negotiated for a better severance package than he had offered at first!

By recognizing our lives are not our own and that there are things we cannot change but only make worse by our bad attitude, we both left at peace and able to continue to relate to former employees with little resentment.

A Prodigal Son's Story: Not Fun but Worth It

William: There were at least three if not four generations of broken fatherhood in my family. My dad and I reached a place where we couldn't even see each other much less talk about where I was at or how to get back together.

My mother told me that she prayed every day for me, and I believe it. I don't think we can ever underestimate the value of prayer.

My parents were open for reconciliation, but it took a lot of humility for both me and my dad; a lot of tears and honest confession on both of our parts. Dad and I had to walk this out together. I wouldn't say that's normal for everybody, but it's how we had to do it.

And what did he do that allowed you to respond? Or did you initiate the process?

I don't think I could make a formula for it. It wasn't a matter of doing at all. It was more a question of: Are we willing to choose the hard road of suffering? I mean, it wasn't fun. But I can tell people it was worth it, battling it out with Dad. To be really honest, I was like, "My flesh hates you but I want to love you and I'm sick of this," and doing it all in tears. That's not fun!

We've come a long way. There's nothing prescriptive about it. It just takes humility and a lot of surrender, forgiveness and perseverance on both sides.

A Traveling Salesman Changes Course

Tell us what happened that created the separation between you and your children?

Dean: There were two factors. I was an authoritarian father and a weekend dad. I would come home and decide that everything had to be done my way. While I was gone, everyone was free to do it their way. But when I was home, my way! I was brought up like that. You do what you are told. If you had an opinion, be quiet about it. I demanded that when I came home.

I was putting all my energy into my career. My children were supposed to just come along and grow up! I was out of town traveling, every day a different city. I didn't have much time to think about my life or what was going on back home. I had to prepare my next visit while traveling all over North America. Busy, busy, busy!

When did you see that something was wrong and what did you do?

During my traveling years, I did make sure they got a good education. I sent my kids to a private school, but one that I really couldn't afford. So I made an arrangement with the headmaster that I would paint classrooms on weekends to help pay their tuition. My children were able to see in a practical way how much I cared for them.

Then, when I stopped traveling and started my own consulting business, I began to realize that I had missed events, both good and bad, with my kids.

My son was in his early teens one night when I was, of course, out of town. He got drunk. A friend of ours had to come over and sit with him all night, with all the vomiting, and help him live through it. When I came home and heard about it, I had a shouting match with my son. It got so heated, he locked himself in the bathroom. I was still furious and went banging on the door so loud, it sounded like a shotgun. On the other side, he was so angry that he punched his fist through the wall!

I didn't realize how significant that moment was for both of us until years later, he told me, "Dad I'm glad you took a stand, because I would have gone the other way. But you held firm and I understood what you meant." Even though I didn't react very well, just being there apparently made a difference for him in that moment.

With each child it was different. Nancy, my daughter, decided to run off with a drug addict in her teen years. I was putting pressure on her to go to college. "Nancy, you need an education!" I was the first of all my relatives to go to college and I insisted how important it was. She tried, but didn't like it, so she rebelled and went off with the druggie.

Every once in a while they would come back to the house. I remember one time she brought him home in this beat-up pickup truck with a skull in front. I blew my top. I was just walking in the door from a trip, saw that out front and yelled, "What is that doing out there? Who's here?" She ran out of the house with him and we didn't hear from them for two whole years! That was a very hard time.

A counselor advised us, "Let her go and pray for her. There's nothing else you can do at this point."

One day, she came back and said, "Dad, I need to go to the storage locker. I need to get his toolset so that we can sell it." I took her there and it was empty. That was a revelation. Whatever her boyfriend had been telling her was a lie. He had sold off everything to buy more drugs. She was devastated.

That's when I just hugged her and we really connected. She knew we were there for her. It started an incredibly strong relationship. Any time she felt uncomfortable after that, she would come to me. It grew to where we could tell each other everything. She knows my business inside out and now, she's running the company!

Some other things happened. My son got his masters in international finance and went to work for a company that was tightly controlled by one family. When that family was out of town, none of the employees could make any decisions. He decided that wasn't for him. He came to me and asked, "Dad, can I work for you for a while and learn about computers?" He ended up working for me for quite a few years. So we got to be together, not in the camping sense, but in an environment of an exchange of ideas. That became the basis for a stronger relationship.

One more thing that keeps our relationship going is sincere and constant affirmation. Like yesterday, my son sent us some money he owed us. I sent him back a text saying, "Thank you, we appreciate it. We can't tell you how much your mother and I love you and are proud of you!" It's not an effort anymore, but just an automatic thing.

Grandparents Get Another Chance

Charles and Cynthia: Two of our children became angry with us and decided they did not want to hear any more of our advice, especially in regard to their dating and eventual marriages. The message we received was basically, "Stay away! We will handle our relationships in our own way, and we don't need you telling us what to do.

What did you do then to break the ice?

When they had kids of their own, things began to change. Our busy, grown children needed help with transportation, babysitting and childcare while they were working. Even though retired and living in Europe, we made a way to come back to the States for at least eight months a year and help with their toddlers any way we could.

Over the years, we were surprised to see our grandkids displaying some of our values they apparently caught from our children, even though our children had rejected us for a time. Our role now was to reinforce these values and compliment our children on their wisdom and discipline! It was like a second chance to be Mom and Dad. During those years, we learned to keep our mouths shut and not judge the behavior of our offspring but love and give sacrificially. We were kinda like their "slaves" for about ten years.

It was also important for us to learn to ask forgiveness of our adult children. Parents make mistakes, but we have learned to imitate the grace that was given to us and pass that along to our children.

Now they have come full circle. The tension has lifted and we are once again appreciated members of their extended families.

What advice would you give grandparents in similar circumstances?

Start with service and love. Words don't always work when the offense is deep.

A Daughter Decides Who She Will Be

Your parents put you into a boarding school early on. How did that affect you?

Martha: On the day of the California Earthquake in 1983, I remember just holding onto a steel railing in terror. It brought back memories of my first day at boarding school.

I was scared to death. I had been dropped off at the school and just hung by the banister rail. I could have screamed my head off, but there was nothing I could do. My parents, my security, everything, was gone. In that moment, I was an only child twelve years of age, suddenly alone in an unfamiliar place.

I had been very sheltered previously. It was us against the world. I didn't go to movies, not even *Peter Pan,* because of the strong spiritual themes. That was my upbringing. Now, I was at an international school with girls from many different backgrounds quite distinct from my own.

From that moment on, it was survival. So I learned survival skills and how to be tough. I was an honors student studying music. My parents, who were actually ministers, never related to what I was doing. They would come and visit maybe for a day, but they never related to my life. I was basically on my own.

Can you think of a time when you were able to bring closure to the feelings you had?

I never had closure with my mother. She died on my birthday while I was on a plane and I didn't get to say good-bye. I remember my feelings when they put her in the ground. I nearly passed out.

In my mid-twenties, I began to look at my mom's background, who she was, her frailties, and I realized she did what she could. I had to let that go. I think she was a good mom when I was a very young child. Things changed as I got older. But I think there comes a point when we have to realize that we are all human beings—fragile and frail. You just have to let go. It really comes down to not so much what they do, but what you decide to do about a given situation. A counselor helped me see it this way: "You know what kind of father or mother they were, now you have to decide what kind of daughter you will be."

A Father Switches Careers to Understand His Son

Anders is a state social worker in Scandinavia who administers methadone (a heroine substitute drug) to recovering addicts. With tears in his eyes, he told us he took this job "because of my son."

Anders: My son developed a drug addiction around 1990 at seventeen-years-old. He started out by smoking cannabis. His personality began to change. Before, he was quite creative, enjoyed singing and painting. Many of his friends really liked him. But he was shy. The marijuana, at first, helped him feel stronger and more confident.

When he moved away to college, he also had to learn to work, so he couldn't spend so much time in drugs. He sang and rapped and was able to make ends meet.

But when he came home, his brothers were not happy with him and his drug habit. As tension rose, we cried out to God and felt like His answer was, "Be open with others around you. Don't carry this alone." He eventually left. It was hard.

We shared the struggle with a few others and learned to tell our story like it is and not with shame. It was not important for us that people feel sorry for us. We shared with others so that they could pray with us.

What do you think helped make the space smaller between you and him after this hard time?

To be honest, it was my relationship with God and having others stand with me. Especially my wife has helped me to continue on. Our marriage is very strong now because we are fighting together.

For me, it's also been helpful to be together with other men. Not necessarily others who have similar problems, just men of confidence to whom I can speak openly and who will also tell me the truth that I need to hear. We have gone on several retreats with just four or five men where we can talk, laugh and cry together. That is helping me so much.

There are times when we don't hear from our son for many months. We don't know where he is living or even if he is still alive. Once, we went to try to find him in Christiania, Denmark, a self-governed kind of hippy utopia, where we heard he was staying. We didn't know if we would see him or not.

We actually met him there. Five months of hearing nothing and then, we finally met him. He was so glad to see us. That was a surprise. I think it was important that we went to his place, the place he wants to be. We didn't want to be there, but we went to him. He was very proud of us and was telling everyone in Christiania, "This is my father and this is my mother." When he would come home sporadically, he never called me his father. He just said, "I am his son." But there, in his place, he called me his father.

I work now with fifty or so recovering addicts whom I serve because they recognize that I know where they are at. I have special compassion for them. It's not easy work, but in a certain way, it helps me feel closer to my son in this difficult stage in his life.

When 2nd Generation Rejects Your Beliefs

Dina: We were surprised when our children rejected our system of beliefs. We didn't expect that because we were working together in camps and charitable service trips once or twice each year. It came to the point of them verbally declaring, "We don't believe what you believe. We don't want to hurt you, Papa and Mama, but we are not there anymore."

This began a hard time of searching our hearts, asking, "What have we done wrong? What's going on?" We started a journey we called, "knocked down, numb, awakened and back to the arena."

Paulo: One thing we learned during this time was to validate their feelings as individuals by listening to what they were saying before correcting them or defending ourselves. We tried hard to remember that young people may not always have the vocabulary to fully express what they think or feel at the time, not until later, even until adulthood.

Can you give us an example or define what you mean by validation?

For instance, if they said something like, "The youth program is bad and all the leaders are fake," we learned to say, "Okay, it sounds like you must have had a really bad experience. Tell us what happened." As they told their story, we would agree with them where we could. We said, "We're very sorry about that. They should not have said or done that to you."

Dina: In one instance one of our children was asked to clean the toilets at a certain camp. When it came time for inspection, he was obliged to kiss the toilet that he had cleaned. If he could not kiss the commode, than it was not clean enough. Because of one or two bad experiences like this, every other memory of good things that happened before literally went down the toilet!

Rather than defending ourselves or the actions of other leaders, we learned to validate our children's feelings and to really listen to what they were saying to keep our respect for them moving in the right direction. We needed not only to hear them, but to recognize when others, whoever they might be, are in the wrong. Leaders are not perfect!

Here's another example. At school, someone was smoking on the property, which was against the rules. The teacher came by and asked, "What's your name?" and the smoker identified herself as our daughter. Later, we received this notice from the school that our daughter was caught smoking on the grounds and this meant a three-day suspension! We knew she smoked and thought it was dumb to do it at school. But she came home and said, "It wasn't me!"

Paulo: It would have been easy to not believe her. But we felt we should just listen. We decided to follow through by going to the school and talking with the responsible teacher. We told him that our daughter said that it wasn't her. Well, the particular teacher replied, "I'm sorry but it was your daughter. She even said so." The school has photos of all the students, so we asked him to show us the girl caught smoking. It wasn't our daughter! The fact that we believed her and followed through brought about more trust in our relationship. We didn't affirm a lot of other things. In those instances we kept our mouths shut. When we could affirm, we did.

Even though their rejection of our faith was painful, we were able to say, "Regardless of faith, you are my child. We don't love you just because you believe the way we do." We had to verbalize many times that they will always be our children and that we will always be their father and mother—no matter what.

Dina: It was both healing and helpful to accept the fact that we were parents of prodigal children who did not have to walk in shame. Bingo! We weren't the only ones! Even our Heavenly Father has billions of them! So we asked Him to teach us how He deals with His broken kids, and not fall into manipulating or threatening them.

Overcoming shame was a big step for us—walking with our heads up, in brokenness but not in defeat, humble but not ashamed. We learned to move past guilt and fear of what others would think or say. A practical way of doing that was to introduce our kids to visitors and friends, affirming their accomplishments before others and showing that we weren't ashamed of them.

What comments have your now-adult children shared with you about that difficult time in their lives?

Paulo: They told us that we did well keeping that channel of communication open and showing that we were proud of them. They have said they felt honored by us and that we didn't impose religion on them as the requirement for communication. We allowed them to think differently while still loving us. Today they will say, "We thank you for the freedom you gave to us."

Any last comments or encouragement to parents who will identify with your experience?

Dina and Paulo: I think one of the phrases that has helped us is, "This is not the last chapter of the book." Keep hope alive. Understand the phase of human development your child is in. Be available, don't shut down. Enjoy your children!

* * * * * * * * * * *

There are likely as many similar stories as there are readers! As one of the testimonies said, "No one get's it right!" (Not even at sixty-years-old!)

I hope these snapshots of reconciliation have been helpful for you.

If you have a personal story of repairing a relationship between generations that you would like to submit for possible inclusion in future editions, please write it down and send it on to: 3gthebook@gmail.com. It can be simple or deathless prose. Just as long as it's true!

Your pain may indeed be gain for others who are fighting on the generational dividing lines.

CHAPTER THIRTEEN

Wrap Up

Of all sad words of tongue or pen, the saddest are these, "It might have been."
-John Greenleaf Whittier

I trust you have been uplifted and inspired as much as I have been while considering these timeless principles, simple as grass, yet as complex as the way chlorophyll, water and sunlight make it green. Where do we begin "greening" our connection with our 2nd and 3rd generations?

A good place to start is by scanning the "3G Activities" in the Addendum of this book. Feel free to apply, adapt, rob or merely chuckle at this random collection of ideas for "living life together" with those you love. They are organized into two broad categories, Family and Leadership Teams. All activities may not apply to you, but if you find one or two workable suggestions, the results will be worth the price of this book!

Then, make a commitment to live your life considering how it materially affects your following generations. We often tell those attending seminars to bend their fingers into a "3G" shape something like this (*figure 3*):

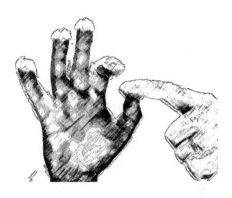

figure 3

We encourage them to form this simple gesture mentally or physically when they are tempted to pass over a teachable moment, avoid that difficult conversation, crowd out family nights with other activities, or even fall into moral temptation. My hope is that fixing on this simple form in your mind or hands may save you from a ruined legacy in moments when it can be hard to choose wisely and well.

Then, start rethinking your personal schedule and time commitments. Are you creating enough space for living life together—the first foundation stone of 3G? If not, what needs to change? Less income but a greater legacy? Making time for family vacations or date nights, even though you don't have time? The positive things about you will not rub off easily on people who don't see you outside of your working mentality. Make those times available. It may be very uncomfortable at first, reconnecting with a teenage daughter or getting to know employees who have never related personally to their boss before. Be intentional! The results will be well worth any initial awkwardness.

Make "open questions" a part of your life skill-set. In your orbit of personal relationships, practice some of the questions listed in chapter nine, or consult a "coaching" website for many more. I predict you will be surprised by how quickly and easily everyday conversations, even conflicts, can open into value discussions and generational transfer.

Consider some of the other practices outlined in this book. Filling up other people's "buckets" with positive affirmation, involving your team in a service project like LifeRice, or serving soup at the local skid-row mission, making stories a fixture of your bedtime routine with your children and your orientation for new employees.

Start somewhere, even with just one new practice: "I will give at least three positive verbal affirmations for any negative comment." "I commit to a date night with my children or spouse (or both) at least once a month." "I will greet my co-workers before explaining the tasks I have for them to do each morning." "I will start with an open how-or-what question rather than a yes-or-no question the next time I confront a child or follower who has failed my expectations." Don't settle for a 1G or 2G lifestyle you'll regret later. Be intentional now.

Here are a few more things to consider as you pack up your 3G duffel bag and start the rest of your amazing journey.

Laughter: Still the Best Medicine

At last, psychologists and authors are including the chuckle as indispensable medicine for emotional health and effective leadership. From the healing clown Dr. Patch Adams[75] to numerous current studies,[76] our modern culture is coming to appreciate the ancient axiom:

> *A merry heart doeth good like a medicine: but a broken spirit drieth the bones. (Proverbs 17:22 KJV)*

There are now AIDS therapies based on a good belly laugh,[77] guffaws advised for stress relief,[78] even a global association for Applied and Therapeutic Humor.[79]

Learning to laugh *at* ourselves and *with* others has been a constant hallmark of our family. I don't think we took this too seriously at first (play on words intended)! As the years passed, all of us began to recognize the value of jokes, puns and light satire to reduce tension, create common space for conversation and remind ourselves that we are only human.

Several years ago, as my mother was in the last stages of a fatal brain cancer, I discovered the source of our family's offbeat but apparently therapeutic tendency to see the lighter side. We knew she had less than ninety days to live, barring a major miracle. Our family members scheduled two-week shifts to make the trek to Kona, Hawaii, and relish the last few moments of her earthly existence. As we reminisced over the important, superfluous and silly memories of a lifetime, she became confined to a wheelchair, then progressively lost the use of motor movements, followed by organ failure and death on March 3, 2010.

Most people would agree that cancer is serious business and nothing to joke about. There were indeed grave moments: grim progress reports, declining bodily functions, insurance and hospital fiascos. We cried rivers. We also were drenched by storms of laughter.

Mom's stoic resistance and positive attitude were amazing, but her sense of humor was insane! She told jokes and revealed mildly vulgar secrets we children never knew about. She shocked us with her levity in the midst of such grievous circumstances.

Things got so hilarious that one night, while Mom, my wife and her mother were carrying on like college freshmen out on the lanai,[80] a neighbor loped across the street to see what was going on.

"I thought someone was supposed to be dying over here!" he declared. "It's like you guys are trying to make death fun!"

A little morbid, but not too far off the mark. Death is an unavoidable part of life. Why not live it to the fullest?

Setbacks, disappointments, failures and successes ... all can be sweetened by well-timed humor. Here's some pertinent advice offered by business consultants Adrian Gostick and Scott Christopher in their book, *The Levity Effect:*

> *Two guys walk into the company coffee corner. One has a big smile and is laughing as he opens the door, the other is straight faced and looking down at the ground as he orders his coffee. Which one's better at his job? You will probably say you need a bit more information, right? Well, current research backs the guy who's laughing and enjoying himself. He is considerably more likely to be more productive, inspiring, engaging, committed, efficient, secure and trusted – an overall better leader.*

> *Humor helps build teams: Humor is the grease in the machine of any team, community or gathering: it smooths interactions, helps everyone to relax, lifts people's spirits and actually moves decisions along. It facilitates a transition from any feeling of tension and defensiveness to a realization of relative safety and playfulness. This is why leaders will do well to create a fun environment in which to relate and work. The leader must lead by example.*[81]

When forced to choose between laughter and crying, choose the chuckle, if you can.

A Decision: Amazing Career or Amazing Family?

There is no escaping the fact that a 3G lifestyle requires time and involvement. There is no way to live experiences together without living experiences together! A little redundant but worth pondering.

If you're good at what you do in any sphere of life, you can easily fill up nights, weekends and vacation time with "important" meetings, communication and activity that will shear off downtime required to transmit your most important values. What needs to give?

We don't live in the '50s. Informal moments together between the generations are not naturally abundant. Where will your priorities be placed?

Consider the following brief histories:

> *In 1876, at 15 years old, young Michel is sent by his father to the penal colony Mettray, a harsh rehabilitation facility for juvenile delinquents. His father, the famous writer Jules Verne, never had much time for Michel. Paradoxically, he was too busy writing novels for young people! The elder Verne decided to impose his authority through an external institution. Their relationship fractured to the point of not talking to each other for years.*

> *In 1994, the Japanese author Kenzaburo Oé was awarded the distinguished Nobel Prize in*

Literature. During his acceptance speech he announced he would no longer be writing novels because he didn't want to create fictional characters any more. He declared to the hushed audience that his life was now dedicated to the only person he was really interested in, his son, Hikari, born with hydrocephalus. Doctors had informed the father at birth that this was an incurable disease and advised he let the newborn die in a special care facility. Kenzabura refused and decided to dedicate the rest of his life to just one task, give voice to this son who could barely speak, who later would become a noted composer of music.

Real stories, radically different results.

The goal is not to lose our personal quest for excellence. No. The quality of your work and the virtue of your interaction with others is what attracts the interest of your children and followers. Don't give up doing well!

> The goal is not to lose our quest for excellence ... Don't give up doing well!

Yet there comes a time when one must decide what is most important: personal glory in this generation or ongoing influence in the next and the next and the next.

I remember well the moment we confronted this momentous decision. Patti and I were in our late twenties. I had visions of our young business, begun in a garage, someday rivaling Bill Hewlett and Dave Packard's start-up. We were on a roll and we were making money!

At first we didn't notice family nights gradually

disappearing off the calendar, mealtimes being cut shorter by meetings and important demands. Like the frog in the proverbial kettle, I was being lured into the myth of the overachiever—the person who is willing to sacrifice relationships and multiplied influence for fleeting glory.

One night, it all became clear and I was faced with a decision. An amazing career or an amazing family? A life dedicated to me or to serving and empowering others?

Time priorities shifted, relationship-building was restored to top priority. I trust that my own children and those business associates, employees and co-workers with whom I've been privileged to walk, appreciate the choice Patti and I made on that decisive night.

Will you be remembered as a career overachiever who used people while building amazing projects, or a 3G achiever who used projects to build amazing people! Will you control your environment to ensure personal success or release others and promote their success? The choice is yours.

One final thought:

> *Very few people say at the end of their lives: Gee,*
> *I wish I had spent more time in the office.*

* * * * * * * * * * *

questions for reflection

- *List five things you could do, starting tomorrow, to begin intentionally influencing the next generation:*

    1.

    2.

    3.

4.

5.

chapter twelve endnotes

[75] Patch Adams was made famous by Robin Williams in the 1998 movie of the same name.

[76] Albert Bottari. *Humor in Healing.*
Rod A. Martin, *Humor, Laughter and Physical Health. Methodological Issues and Research Findings, 2001, etc.*

[77] Ross Seligsen and Karen Peterson. *AIDS Prevention and Treatment: Hope, Humor and Healing. 1992*

[78] *Stress Relief from Laughter? It's no joke.* !http://www.mayoclinic.org/healthy-lifestyle/stress-management/in-depth/stress-relief/art-20044456

[79] http://www.aath.org/

[80] Hawaiian for porch

[81] Adrian Gostick and Scott Christopher. *The Levity Effect: Why it Pays to Lighten Up (2008)*

DID YOU ENJOY THIS BOOK?

ARE THERE OTHERS WHO WOULD APPRECIATE THIS GUIDE FOR THEIR OWN 3G JOURNEY?

You can order additional copies of *3G: The Art of Living Beyond Your Life* on any Amazon website including: www.amazon.com, .de, .es, .co.uk, .fr, etc. Or you can capture this qr image on your mobile phone to go directly to the amazon.com page.

Special discount for bulk orders

For orders of 10 copies or more, wholesale and bookseller inquiries, contact the author directly at:

3gthebook@gmail.com

Acknowledgements

As with anything worthwhile, there are numerous contributors to the content and form of this project. At the risk of passing over many, I will attempt to name a few:

I'm deeply indebted to Dale Kauffman, Christoph Leu, and Guy and Joële Zeller, KKI global leaders, for their patient teaching and modeling of principles that have shaped my thinking. Loren Cunningham, founder of Youth With A Mission, is a contemporary hero to millions and still on the top of my list. I'm very thankful for Erin Healy's patience and professional editing skills, for Penn Clark's additional advice, for Lisa Samson's careful proofreading and for Calvin Hanson and Karen Carrera's graphic art talent displayed in cover designs.

I appreciate the kind coffee bar personnel at the Barcelona Four Points Sheraton who allowed me to sequester a table for eight to ten hours at a time.

I can't leave out the support of our Project: Spain board: Tom Baker, Rich Clewett, Matt Spaulding, Bob Leonard, and Penn Clark, as well as the Iglesia Lokal, in Barcelona for allowing me to free up the time necessary to write.

I wouldn't have anything to say without my wife Patti and our own "2G"—our four children: Kari, Kenny, Kindra and Cristina, along with an extended family of thousands of Spanish and international young people who accompanied our 3G journey. Thanks for allowing me to share your stories.

Finally, thanks to Jesus, the Source, the "zero-G", if you will, for letting me be part of His inheritance!

bibliography/works cited

chapter 1

Wojciechowski, Robert. *Clinical Genetics.* http://
www.ncbi.nlm.nih.gov/pmc/articles/PMC3058260/

chapter 2

Rowe, C. J. *Plato.* Brighton. St. Martin's Press. 1984.

Plato. *Lysis.* translated by Benjamin Jowett. New York.
Scribner's Sons, 1871

University of Chicago Law School. *The Socratic Method
(Green Bag Article).* http://www.law.uchicago.edu/
socrates/soc_article.html

Aristotle, http://www.philosophers.co.uk/aristotle.html

Academy of Plato. http://www-history.mcs.st-andrews.ac.uk/
Societies/Plato.html

Boeree, C. George. *Socrates, Plato and Aristotle.* http://
webspace.ship.edu/cgboer/athenians.html

Chermiss, H. *The Riddle of the Early Academy. New York.
Garland Pub. (1980).*

O'Connor, J.J. and Robertson, E.F. *Biography of Plato.* http://
www-groups.dcs.st-and.ac.uk/~history/Biographies/
Plato.html

Fox, Robin Lane. *Alexander the Great.* New York. E-P. Dutton,
1974.

What Was Abraham's Religion before God Called Him? http://
www.gotquestions.org/Abraham-religion.html

Mount Moriah, Site of the Temple Mount in Jerusalem. http://
www.templemount.org/moriah2.html

Storytelling and Spirituality in Judaism. http://
www.hasidicstories.com/Articles/Hasidic_Theories/
spirit.html

How Old Was Isaac When God Asked Abraham to Sacrifice Him? http://www.biblestudy.org/question/how-old-was-issac-when-god-asked-abraham-to-sacrifice-him.html

Do the Sons Bear the Sins of Their Fathers or Not? https://carm.org/bible-difficulties/genesis-deuteronomy/do-sons-bear-sins-fathers-or-not

The Bible Journey. http://www.thebiblejourney.org/biblejourney2/23-the-journeys-of-adam-enoch-noah-abraham/abrams-journey-to-canaan/

The Journey of Abraham. http://www.kidsbiblemaps.com/abrahams-journey.html

Foreshadowing of Jesus' Resurrection Through Isaac on Mount Moriah. http://www.examiner.com/article/foreshadowing-of-jesus-resurrection-through-isaac-on-mt-moriah

Why Did God Order Abraham to Do Child Sacrifice? http://christianthinktank.com/qkilisak.html

What Were Abraham's Ten Tests? http://www.chabad.org/library/article_cdo/aid/1324268/jewish/What-Were-Abrahams-10-Tests.htm

chapter 4

How to Be Jesus' Disciple: A Vision for Discipleship. http://www.focusequip.org/assets/pdf/how-to-discipleship-vision-preview.pdf

chapter 5

Hunter, James C. *The Servant.* New York. Crown Business, 1998

Dobson, James C. *The New Dare to Discipline.* Carol Stream, IL. Tyndale,1996

Cloud, Henry and Townsend, John. *Boundaries with Kids: When to Say Yes, When to Say No, to Help Your Children Gain Control of Their Lives.* Grand Rapids. *Zondervan, 2001*

Cloud, Henry. *Boundaries for Leaders: Results, Relationships and Being Ridiculously in Charge.* New York. Harper Business, 2013

chapter 6

The Birds and the Bees: Talking to Your Kids About Sex. https://powertochange.com/family/talkkids/

VanCley, Mary. *How to Talk to Your Child About Sex (Ages 6 to 8).* http://www.babycenter.com/0_how-to-talk-to-your-child-about-sex-ages-6-to-8_67908.bc

Gorney, Cynthia. *How to Talk to Your Child about Sex (Ages 6-12).* https://consumer.healthday.com/encyclopedia/children-s-health-10/child-development-news-124/how-to-talk-to-your-child-about-sex-ages-6-to-12-645918.html

chapter 7

Dohrenwend, Robert. *The Sling: Forgotten Firepower of Antiquity.* Journal of Asian Martial Arts, Volume 11 Number 2 – 2002.

Arp, Dave and Claudia. *Giant Steps.* Article in *Christian Parenting Today,* May/June issue. 1994.

Valles, Michael A. *Your Complete Guide to Leaving an Inheritance for Your Children and Others.* Ocala, FL. Atlantic Publishing, 2008.

chapter 8

Elkhorne, J.L. *Edison—The Fabulous Drone, in 73.* Vol. XLVI, No. 3 (March 1967), p. 52

Impact, Small Interactions. http://www.gallup.com/businessjournal/12916/big-impact-small-interactions.aspx

Positive Negative Ratio. http://www.ocde.us/PBIS/Documents/Articles/Positive+$!26+Negative+Ratio.pdf

Zenger, Jack and Folkman, *Joseph. The Ideal Praise to Criticism Ratio.* Harvard Business Review, 2013 https://hbr.org/2013/03/the-ideal-praise-to-criticism

Clifton, Donald O. and Rath, Tom. *How Full Is Your Bucket?* New York. Gallup Press, 2004

La Vanguardia. *Hay que tener fe porque cada día es un nuevo concierto.* http://www.lavanguardia.com/cultura/20160707/403015624216/hay-que-tener-fe-porque-cada-dia-es-un-nuevo-concierto.html

Silk, Danny, ed. *Loving Our Kids on Purpose.* Shippenburg, PA. Destiny Image, 2013

chapter 9

The Older Population: 2010 (PDF). US Census Bureau. November 2011.

Young, William P. *How to Parent by Participation.* http://wmpaulyoung.com/parent-by-participation/

Strauss, William and Howe, Neil. *Generations: The History of America's Future, 1584 to 2069.* New York. William Morrow & Company, 1991.

Strauss, William and Howe, Neil. *Millenials Rising: The Next Great Generation,* New York. Random House, 2000

Adelson, Hal and Ledeen, Ken and Lewis, Harry. *Blown to Bits: Your Life Liberty and Hapiness After the Digital Explosion.* USA R.R. Donnely, 2008.

chapter 10

Robbins, Tony. *Power of Questions.* https://www.tonyrobbins.com/training/power-of-questions/

London, Bianca. *Families only manage to sit down together for dinner twice a week - with 10% NEVER eating together.* Mail Online, Nov 19, 2012. http://www.dailymail.co.uk/femail/article-2235161/Families-manage-sit-dinner-twice-week--10-NEVER-eating-together.html#ixzz4MK16JB3C

Sweat, Rebecca. *The Family That Eats Together.* Vision Media, Fall 2002. https://www.vision.org/visionmedia/article.aspx%3Fid%3D246

The Importance of Family Dinners. Center on Addiction. Sep 2012. http://www.centeronaddiction.org/addiction-research/reports/importance-of-family-dinners-2012

Watson, Brad A. *Theology of Food.* May 26, 2016. http://bradawatson.com/2016/05/eating-together/

Chester, Tim. *Show Hospitality and Share the Gospel.* GCD, Feb 6, 2012. http://gcdiscipleship.com/2012/02/06/show-hospitality-share-the-gospel/

chapter 11

de Chartres, Bernard. *We Are Like Dwarfs on the Shoulders of Giants.* http://www.goodreads.com/quotes/526239-we-are-like-dwarfs-on-the-shoulders-of-giants-so

chapter 13

Whittier, John Greenleaf. *Maud Muller.* Yale Book of American Verse, http://www.bartleby.com/102/76.html

Albert Bottari. *Humor in Healing.* http://www.robertottohypnosis.com/resources/articles/humorinhealing.pdf

Rod A. Martin, *Humor, Laughter and Physical Health. Methodological Issues and Research Findings, 2001, etc.*

Ross Seligsen and Karen Peterson. *AIDS Prevention and Treatment: Hope, Humor and Healing.* 1992

Stress Relief from Laughter? It's no joke. http://www.mayoclinic.org/healthy-lifestyle/stress-management/in-depth/stress-relief/art-20044456

Gostick, Adrian and Christopher, Scott. *The Levity Effect: Why It Pays to Lighten Up.* Hoboken, NJ. Wiley & Sons, 2008

Addendum 1

Twenty-one 3G Ideas for Families and Leadership Teams

FAMILIES

1. Take a family vacation and don't take electronic devices with you for at least part of the time.

2. Take a child to work with you for a whole day.

3. Design together a set of "challenges" as a rite of passage into the teenage years. (See last part of chapter six.)

4. Start a habit of giving one verbal affirmation per day to your spouse and children. They will notice the difference!

5. Schedule agreed-upon times at least twice per week for families to eat together.

6. Ask grandparents to speak/pray over the lives of their grandchildren during a future family visit. Give them some lead time to think about what they will say or pray.

7. Learn how to do something you have never done together with one or more children. Examples: bake a cake, plant a garden, play guitar, ride a Jet Ski, rock climb. It's great for them to see you also in a learning curve.

8. Plan a date night once month with your children. Go to a restaurant of their choice with no particular agenda except finding out what they are learning about life.

9. Learn some phrases and name of objects in a language none of you know or of a place you will be going soon. Put up stickers around the house that show the name of the object in the new language and try to use these words and phrases at family meal times.

10. Tell your children the "love story" of how you met your spouse.

11. On their birthday, tell your children the story of when they were born. Make it a fun story they will never forget by acting it out with props.

12. Build a Family Shield together. As the medieval knights had shields showing symbols of their heritage, such as castles or lions, decide together what are the most important four or five values that describe your family or group. Then, using colored paper, silver pens, tape, glue, gatorboard, paint, whatever, make a mixed-media artistic creation in the shape of a shield that exemplifies those values.

13. Pick a favorite TV gameshow and adapt it for a fun family activity. Our favorites were *Family Feud,* guessing other's answers to questions like, "What is a common one-word greeting?" Use answers from the family or from a quick survey of friends. We also liked to play *American Gladiators*, where each person had to walk across a plank set a few inches off the ground in the living room while being pounded with pillows, Nerf balls and towels.

14. Go on a family mission trip locally or internationally. Or pack up meals to send to needy areas of the world. (See reference to *Liferice.org* in Chapter eight).

15. Play walking games when out strolling. Our favorite was *George of the Jungle*. We would sing the theme song, "George, George, George of the Jungle, Strong as he could be. Oh uoh, oh uoh, watch out for that tree!" and then nudge the other toward a nearby post or tree along the way. Just don't get carried away and hurt anyone!

16. Celebrate the family milestones, not just birthdays. A new house, your child's first job, a driver's license—do something special, cherish the moment.

17. Initiate a retro-night where no TV, social media, computer games or video are allowed for a two-to four-hour period. Make it fun by having special food or snacks. Everyone can read a book or play table games or whatever.

18. Ask your children regularly, "Are you having a happy childhood?"

19. Ask children what they would like to eat. Then search out recipes and shop for ingredients together.

20. Build a set of household tasks beyond normal chores, which can receive payment or prizes: doing the windows, ironing, moving rocks, cleaning the garage.

21. Specifically and verbally praise your child for a job well done in some area or for some attitude shown.

LEADERSHIP TEAMS

1. Learn to "greet the person first" with questions like, "How are you doing today?" "How was that trip to Mexico over the weekend?" before assigning or evaluating work.

2. Commit yourself to reviewing/evaluating events with subordinates immediately after any new major task: leading a team meeting, speaking in public, building a new widget.

3. Try using these review/evaluation questions: a.)What went well? (Let them answer and then add as many other positive observations as you can) b.) What could you do even better? c.)What practical steps can you take to achieve that excellence?

4. Take your whole staff or work team out for a long lunch just because you want to.

5. Intentionally take an associate or staff member with you to a conference above their normal level of involvement.

6. Purposely introduce your associates and team members to "important" people that you know or happen by your workplace.

7. Take time to go through a complete "discipleship cycle" when giving employees a new task: 1. You demonstrate how to do it while they watch; 2. You help them do it; 3. You observe while they do it; 4. They do it and start teaching others.

8. Play "work bingo" by filling in a square each time your team completes a task or achieves a goal. When a manager has signed off on five in a row, the employee or team wins a prize.

9. When reaching a major goal, have leaders cook a special breakfast for team members.

10. Plan a float trip together down a local river or creek.

11. Take your team out to do a fun physical activity: go-cart racing, zip-lining, stand-up paddle boarding, sledding.

12. Do something special for an employee's family.

13. Do something fun to greet new employees. Put up a poster and balloons, play fanfare music when they arrive.

14. (In the US) Have a "bracketing pool" for March Madness NCAA basketball tournaments. Give a prize for the best and the worst brackets.

15. Have a "Bring your kids to work" day with special tours and demos.

16. Have an "Office Olympics" with events made out of office items: rubber-band toss, maximum swivel-chair rotation, paper-ball wastebasket shooting.

17. Hold meetings away from your normal meeting room.

18. Use the "sandwich method" (two pieces of bread with salami in between) whenever correction or redirection is required. Start with praise and positive observations: "Paul, you are one of the most creative and spontaneous people on our team." Then comes the "salami," the area needing correction: "However, borrowing everyone's mobile phone and leaving a picture of yourself on the screensaver may have been an intrusion into the privacy of some." After discussing steps to correct the situation, end with another slice of "bread": "We're so glad to have you on our team. In fact, I am looking for some jokes to lighten up my next management talk. Would you like to suggest a few?"

19. Take your staff or team on a two-to three-day planning retreat in a nice place with ample time for relaxation and games in between sessions.

20. Ask employees regularly, "What do you need to do your job better?" and provide what they suggest to the best of your or your organization's ability.

21. Put up a Wall of Fame with newspaper clippings, pictures, cards, and so on of organization events and individual accomplishments.

Made in the USA
Columbia, SC
27 July 2020